THE POWER OF MENTAL TOUGHNESS

DISCOVER HOW TO BUILD MENTAL TOUGHNESS AND CONTROL YOUR THOUGHTS IN ORDER TO ACHIEVE AT THE HIGHEST LEVELS

WILLIAM ANDERSON

CONTENTS

INTRODUCTION

To succeed, you need mental toughness: the confidence and resilience of an individual that indicates how influential he or she may be at work, in personal relationships, and in education. In addition, you need grit, which describes someone who has a strong sense of character.

How often have you pictured a life that is more substantial than the one you are living? There is something holding you back from reaching your potential and making choices that impact your life in a positive way. It's easy to feel that life is unfair and there is little you can do to change it—that you are stuck in a loop of one step forward and then one enormous landslide backward.

I grew up in Romania, an ex-communist country. The revolution took place in 1989 and I was born in 1996 into a country that was already poor. My parents could afford very little while caring for six children on my father's salary. I always dreamed big and wanted to dedicate my life to something meaningful. I wanted to play professional soccer in Europe, but since we didn't have the money to send me to a city where I could join a team to fulfill my goal, I was forced to let this dream go.

Schoolwork wasn't my strength since I found it difficult to focus—I later discovered that I had ADHD. At age 18, I saw a fitness influencer, Jeff Seid, who was so motivated and dedicated to his elite fitness. I was inspired to become a fitness influencer as well. I said goodbye to Romania and moved to several countries throughout Europe to chase my dream, all while working up to 12 hours a day. At the same time, I was working out early in the morning, and waking up at 3 AM. I made all of these sacrifices to obtain the PRO CARD in the Men's Physique Division.

After several injuries and my body giving up on me despite my drive, I went back to Romania and, with much hard work, began a business that eventually made a profit. This success, through all my failings and getting back up, made me realize that my true path led me to write this book to encourage others to never give up on making something meaningful of their goals, of their lives.

The difficulty doesn't always lie in knowing what you want to get out of life, but in knowing how to achieve the goals and standards that you have set out for yourself. Dreams and goals are not achieved by putting them out into the universe or wishing on a double rainbow. They are achieved by becoming mentally prepared for hard work and by using the power of mental toughness to build your life to the highest level of success.

The secret to success? It's all in your mind.

Your ability to do great things lies in your ability to convince yourself that you can achieve greatness. Mental strength is a concept that relates directly to traits associated with and interchangeable with persistence, strength, resilience (Cleveland Clinic, 2022), emotional regulation, and a positive outlook. All of these qualities will help establish how likely you are to visualize and bring to fruition your dreams.

Through this book, I will guide you toward realizing your inner strength and how to increase your mental toughness so that you can reach your goals through hard work, planning, and self-realization. Mental toughness can be improved through

- establishing pertinent goals.

- abiding by your body's needs.

- focusing on meaningful tasks and projects.

- acknowledging and healing feelings of negativity.

- pushing beyond your comfort zone.

Mental toughness is key to achieving your goals in life, including work, home life, and health goals. You will learn that there is more to setting up and establishing your goals than planning, but hard work and the ability to repel negative energy from others will help set the stage for how your life plays out.

You will learn what mental toughness is, where it comes from, and why it is crucial for your success. You will learn that mental strength has no poster child and that anyone is capable, not only those who appear rugged, and why today's generation and accessibility to social media is breeding self-pity and a lazier outlook on what it takes to earn your worth.

Everyone is traveling a different journey through this life; where we end up is determined by the effort we put in and the risks we take as we go along. There are battles that you will face and times that you will want to give up, so you will learn how to use the storms to reap lusher rewards and use the broken pieces of shattered dreams and the chants of naysayers to build a life from the mosaic of broken glass.

Many components of life take mental toughness and everyone is capable of hard work. Whether you are building your dream business, working through university, joining the military, or saving up to buy your first home, you will get there through determination and grit.

Acknowledge that your journey will be challenging and then set out knowing that you will have to break down walls, including your own, to make things happen. Associate with like-minded people who are building their own mental strength and who accept that their failures can be overcome through their own determination.

While you read through this journey to mental toughness, use a pencil to make notes or highlight key components that you want to revisit later. If you like to keep your books free of markings, use sticky notes or fold the corners of the pages to find notable points later on. If you have the ebook, grab a pad of paper and make key notes as you go along.

The power of mental toughness is a journey that begins now.

1

WHAT IS MENTAL TOUGHNESS AND WHERE DOES IT COME FROM

Mental toughness refers to someone who is comfortable with who they are and can take the challenges that life throws at them with ease. Mental toughness isn't to be confused with arrogance or narcissism, but rather the confidence that one has in their ability to succeed, even when things seem insurmountable.

Building mental toughness or mental strength is essential to living your life to the fullest. Developing your mental health, using a variety of tools and various techniques will allow you to push for what you truly want and not let obstacles scare you off of your chosen path.

In addition to building meaningful connections with others and building self-esteem, strong mental strength gives us the courage to try things that frighten us and allows us to cope with challenging events and situations that occur in life.

Mental health is largely similar to mental strength but they are, in fact, different.

You know what mental strength is but you may not know that mental health is defined as one's emotional well-being. However, even if you do not suffer from depression, anxiety, or another form of mental illness, you may not have mental toughness. In fact, you may have anxiety and struggle with depression but be a mentally strong individual. To break it down:

Mental health is

- having a mental health issue or the absence of a mental health issue.

- your state of mental well-being overall.

Mental strength is

- having a grip on and understanding of your emotions.

- being able to handle negative situations in a positive way.

- knowing when to indulge your emotions and the ability to set them aside.

The idea behind mental toughness is to be strong when faced with adversity, but this is not something that we all can do. Mental strength takes consistent work, challenging yourself, and not letting anyone else get into your head.

Emotional regulation is key to mental toughness because it allows us to exercise control over our emotions. To have emotional regulation is to have the ability to challenge the situation we are in and rethink the outcome and what we can do to get there. It requires us to control our anger, anxiety, and fear, and refocus our thoughts in a more productive manner.

HOW TO BUILD YOUR MENTAL TOUGHNESS

Everyone, with determination, is capable of gaining mental toughness. Just as consistent exercises are necessary to help shape and strengthen your muscles to withstand injury, mental toughness can be built through a series of mental exercises.

COGNITIVE EXERCISES

These allow you to change your way of thinking by way of establishing a mindset that helps you maintain a positive outlook and rework any negative thoughts or reinvent a realistic mindset from one of self-doubt. Some ways to establish and practice cognitive exercises may include (Cleveland Clinic, 2022):

- Keeping a gratitude diary that acknowledges what you have and affirms feelings of positivity and thoughts of gratitude.

- Argue for the opposition when you find yourself dwelling on all that could go wrong. Instead, consider all that could go exactly as you have planned for it to go.

- Empathize with yourself and offer compassion to yourself when mistakes are made, as you would a friend. We are often much harder on ourselves than we would be on anyone that we consider a loved one.

EMOTIONAL EXERCISES

These exercises help heighten your awareness of your emotional position and give you the ability to see it as useful. These may help you to manage uncomfortable feelings or reduce the magnitude of negative emotions or those that cause ill effects. These exercises can be:

- Labeling how you feel so that you can take a step back and see them from a different perspective. This may allow you to see your emotions for what they are and help alleviate the darkness they have over you. Rather than focusing on negative feelings, change your mindset by going for a walk in the fresh air or allow yourself to say the feeling out loud but then reaffirm that you are not what those feelings imply.

BEHAVIORAL EXERCISES

These include doing what will help you feel your best and allow you to live your best and happiest life. There are some behavioral exercises you can do.

Schedule positive activities to do for yourself, with or without someone else. This can be anything from having a spa day to reading a book or going paddleboarding. Anything that reaffirms that you are alive and doing well while also giving you some much-needed self-reflection, is going to help you realize that you are worth your accomplishments.

There are three essential components to building your mental toughness:

1. Realistic Thinking

   Realistic thinking is critical to mental toughness because it demonstrates the ability to recognize irrational thoughts and reimagine them as more pragmatic concepts. This reasoning allows you to recognize when you are being critical of your efforts or emotions and rework your inner voice to be more compassionate.

2. Acknowledging Your Feelings

   Having mental strength is not about being above pain or holding back emotions, but rather acknowledging how you are feeling and understanding why. The ability to take a deep breath and accept that you are feeling unpleasant is a sign of mental toughness.

3. Taking Positive Action

   A great sign of mental toughness is taking productive steps toward affirmative action in your goals or even with self-care. This refers to anything that moves you toward making your life more positive.

WAYS TO BUILD MENTAL STRENGTH

Mental toughness is a key component to the success of elite athletes, entrepreneurs, doctors, nurses, paramedics, firemen, police officers, writers, teachers, parents, and so on. To become successful in any one of these professions or in raising a family, you need to have grit, determination, and a will to overcome all odds.

Striving to achieve mental toughness and persevere is a notable goal and the concept is understandable, but what does mental strength look like every day?

Elite athletes that are mentally strong are consistent and resilient. They hit their workouts without fail, push themselves past their limits, and always support those around them.

Community and business leaders strive to get the job done, be consistent, and set clear and attainable goals that they strive for every day. Negative comments and challenging times do not prevent them from moving forward toward their goals and they encourage others to stay the course along their own paths to success. These leaders build others up because they understand there is strength in supporting others.

Editors, writers, and other artists are consistent in the schedules they keep and the deadlines they face. They are committed to doing a good job and set out to do a good job in the time they have allotted. I would not have been able to write this book without the inspiration to put together a concise plan and the determination to follow through.

Having perseverance and determination doesn't need to be something you took to from the time you were a child; it can be earned by developing mental toughness. Some strategies that are effective in building mental toughness in life include:

DEFINING WHAT MENTAL TOUGHNESS MEANS TO YOU

Everyone has their own definition of what it means to be mentally tough. To an athlete, it might be rebuilding after an injury, but to you it might mean

- eating a clean diet for a month to help lose weight.

- adding a repetition to your workout every week to build up muscle mass.

- taking a night class to help you change careers.

- beating a work deadline rather than aiming to get it done right on time.

Set a clear idea about the goal you set for yourself. While being mentally strong is abstract and different for everyone, it is how we build a stronger connection to tangible actions.

BUILDING MENTAL TOUGHNESS

Applying mental strength to exceptional circumstances isn't the only way to build strength. It isn't only about coming back from a devastating loss or buying your first house after you lose everything. These extreme circumstances absolutely build perseverance and strengthen resolve, but they are not the only thing that builds mental strength.

Small, everyday challenges and wins help build mental toughness, as working out every day and gradually building your muscles are going to build a stronger base than running a triathlon every three months without preparation.

Showing yourself that you can do one more pull-up, walk one more mile, and put in an extra hour a day to finish a house project will help build up confidence in yourself and prove that you are capable every day—not only when all the chips are down.

FINDING THE ROOTS OF MENTAL TOUGHNESS

Mental toughness comes from habits, not impulses. Being strong, mentally, isn't about pulling on a cape and entering superhero mode on the odd occasion it is necessary; it's about consistently sticking to your schedule or steamrolling challenges time and again. Those who are mentally tough do not need an abundance of courage or necessarily have the brains to attend Yale University—they need habits that build a foundation of reliance.

You can build mental strength through cognitive, emotional, and behavioral exercises. Building mental strength will help you become less likely to adapt to the expectation of others and fall into negative comments. Mental toughness will help you make thought-out, intentional decisions that will benefit you on your path to a better life.

CHALLENGE YOURSELF: INCREASE TOUGH THINKING

A strong mind is needed for mental toughness. A strong mind allows you to control your thoughts, have positive self-talk, and stay in a mindset that makes thriving much easier. To maintain this positive mindset, you need to acknowledge when you are caught in a negative thought pattern so you can use learned techniques to redirect your thinking to positive action.

The ability to recognize negative thinking will allow you to reset to positive thoughts and manage your emotions. When you identify negativity creeping in, you can establish boundaries within yourself to help you turn it into useful thinking.

The exercise that you need to practice is called thought-stopping. This is the action of suppressing undesirable thoughts and acts as a way to disrupt a pattern of negative thinking and direct your efforts and thoughts into something that helps alleviate stress and not induce it, with the goal of preventing unhelpful behaviors from triggering you in the first place.

The first step is to acknowledge when your thoughts are turning negative. The second step allows you to choose from one of three options:

1. Instantly imagine a flashing red light.

2. Instantly tell yourself to stop.

3. Instantly do both.

These simple steps will defer the negative thought and reset your way of thinking to a more constructive solution.

KEY TAKEAWAYS

In this chapter, you learned that:

- building mental toughness or mental strength is essential to living your life to the fullest.

- there are three essential components to building your mental toughness–realistic thinking, acknowledging your feelings, and taking positive action.

- mental strength can be built through cognitive, emotional, and behavioral exercises. Building mental strength will help you become less likely to adapt to the expectation of others and fall into negative comments.

2

WHY BEING MENTALLY TOUGH IS SO IMPORTANT

W e are all born with the potential to be mentally tough, but it takes perseverance and a sense of urgency. Being mentally tough is a mindset that can be taught and learned by anyone. People who have earned mental strength have attributes that lead to them being more successful, such as being more determined, showing consistency, and reaping better results in their job, personal life, and goals. Other benefits include (Yeong, 2017):

1. Feeling of contentment

   When you have mental toughness you are more likely to feel content in life, have less stress, not struggle with mental health illness, and to rest better at night. Those who are mentally tough are less likely to let others get away with bullying them because they know their worth.

2. Aspiration and perseverance

   When you are mentally tough, you are able to handle more stress, which means you push yourself beyond your comfort zone. It will help you overcome a lack of purpose and urge you to keep going when your mind is trying to convince you to surrender your ambition.

3. Positive outlook

   Those who possess mental strength have a more positive attitude and a more hopeful outlook on how well things can turn out. They are also more likely to try new activities and extend their abilities to volunteering and helping to provide a more positive environment for others.

4. Greater performance

   With mental strength comes the confidence to deliver on expectations of oneself, which extends to social commitments and relationships, as well as producing more output in these areas.

   When you are mentally strong, you will be more confident in your work, have firm boundaries in relationships, and be more reliable in general because mentally tough people do not pull out of obligations.

5. Greater self-worth

   No one is immune to feeling inadequate or questioning their ability from time to time, but it is mental strength that keeps those feelings from overtaking your potential. When your own mind is challenging your ability, it's not always easy to overcome, but when you are prepared, you are able to ignore the negativity that swirls in your head and persevere.

6. Use failures as strength

Any failure can be saddled with feelings of awkwardness or embarrassment which can deter many from carrying on with their goals. With mental strength comes the ability to take failure and transform the negative into stepping stones to avoid entering into the patterns or decisions that lead to the same mistakes. Failure breeds learning opportunities and should be collected and moved on.

7. Helps refute negativity

There are those who believe they know everything, even what's best for you. Mental toughness helps reject bad advice that others may offer. Feeling confident in your self-worth will help take negative criticism and set it aside rather than carry it alongside you. You will feel confident enough to move on without debating the issues someone may have.

DAILY HABITS THAT WILL IMPROVE MENTAL STRENGTH

Mental strength, as mentioned, is not something you are born with or will come into naturally by going through adversity. Just as you need to exercise to build your physical strength, building mental strength happens over time with consistency and habit-building.

Some habits that will help you build your mental toughness include:

1. Express thanks: Remind yourself to be thankful every day for what you have, without focusing on the negative. By acknowledging the things you are grateful for—whether by writing it in a journal, saying it as a daily affirmation, or thinking to yourself—you are pushing out any negative thoughts that can bog down the mind.

2. Shut out all distractions: Take fifteen minutes each day to sit and be with your own thoughts. Sitting in the silence of your own space and shutting out all distractions is essential to building mental toughness.

3. Push beyond your comfort zone: Take the time every day to push yourself beyond what is easy or comfortable. Going to the gym even though you feel tired, asking for an assignment at work that you really want, or asserting yourself at the

forefront of a conversation will all help to build your confidence and help prove to yourself that you are willing to do what once seemed out of reach.

4. Take responsibility for yourself: Blaming others for your unfortunate circumstances is going to keep you stuck in a place of self-pity. Rather than using language such as, "my friends make me feel inadequate," choose to rephrase it as, "I am the one who controls how I feel."

5. Treat yourself with kindness: Instigating a kind and supportive inner voice creates a sense of self-compassion. Speak to yourself as you would if you were speaking to a friend and be encouraging rather than critical. Your inner voice should also be strong enough to put you in check if you are sliding into self-loathing or avoiding accountability for your actions.

6. Acknowledge and identify your feelings: It should be a daily habit to address your feelings–good and bad–to determine how they may be affecting the choices you make. Making choices that will have a negative impact can occur when we allow our feelings to run rampant without considering how the highest highs or the lowest lows may affect our decision.

7. Utilize your mental energy productively: Wasting time on things that occurred in the past or worrying about an outcome that you have no control over will take an emotional toll and waste your time. Save your mental energy for things that you can solve and for reframing the negative into a positive solution or next step.

You now know that mental toughness is the ability to perform optimally on a consistent basis in any situation that you find yourself in. You don't have to be at the top level of your sport, business, or whatever else you are climbing toward to have mental toughness.

Mental toughness is what will get you ahead in any aspect of your life that you strive to do better in. Building habits that strengthen your mental toughness is key to fulfilling your goals. Below are some exercises that can help you improve your mental toughness.

EXERCISES THAT WILL HELP IMPROVE YOUR MENTAL TOUGHNESS

Just as an elite athlete needs to consistently practice to build their muscle memory in their sport of choice, mental toughness can only be strengthened through consistent work and dedication to making decisions that will lead to your goals.

There are daily exercises that can be done to improve your mental toughness. With practice, these techniques will help you overcome mental weakness without even thinking about it.

Visualize the outcome you want: Those with uncertain thoughts know what it's like to wake up and go to bed with the same lingering thoughts–Did I perform well enough for the promotion? Will I get the job or did I blow the interview? Am I raising happy children?

Take those negative and nagging thoughts and turn them into optimistic phrases that encourage a more positive outcome–the best scenario there could be. You may think that this is a sure way to build up hope only to be met with disappointment if things don't work out, but it's not the case. Building a positive expectation will help you build the mental expectation that you are capable and deserving of good things. Envisioning a positive outcome will create more chances of greatness than negativity.

Make anxiety work for you: Malleability is what allows our brains to be resilient when we go through difficulties. It is the reason we are able to take a breath, assess the situation, and rethink our decisions and thoughts to make more calculated decisions. Remind yourself that anxiety is not necessarily a detriment.

- Anger can hinder our performance and progress or it can sharpen our aim, improve our accessibility to motivating thoughts, and give clarity to what should come first.

- Sadness can deflate our motivation or it can reignite motivation that will lead to changes and strength in our behavior and help us change our circumstances or environment.

- Worrying about failure can lead to avoidance of effort to accomplish your goals or it can help you set more distinguished steps to move you along your path with more achievable goals and help you narrow your motivation.

- Fear is a powerful deterrent when you allow it to remind you of what you failed to accomplish or you can use it to learn from your mistakes and redirect yourself to other opportunities.

- Disappointment can rob you of motivation or light a fire that will challenge you to do better or try to do more.

When broken down, these may seem like simple examples, but engaging in these practices will help lead you to concrete choices that create concrete outcomes.

Get outdoors: Research has proven that getting back to nature has powerful effects on improving the quality of our mental health and resilience. Spending time on mountain trails, on the water, or going for a walk in the park will all lift your spirits and create a bond with nature which increases serotonin levels and helps restore energy and balance your equilibrium.

Recognize your support network: Building mental toughness is reliant on having a support network of family and friends that will be there to help support you through challenging times. Knowing that someone is there when you need them will lessen anxiety.

When you are feeling distressed, it is easy to hide inside yourself and withdraw from those around you, social activities, and your goals. When you know you have someone backing you, it offers confidence and a push to carry on, even in the most trying times.

Habitual practices and daily exercises will help you build your mental toughness. By using visualization techniques and simple meditation or getting outdoors, you can clear your mind of the negative, making room for productive thoughts.

If someone talks about a goal they want to accomplish but then follows up with, "But I don't have time," that is weakness talking. If you have something important to you, you will make the time; that is mental strength.

There is a hospice in Vancouver, Canada, called Canuck Place Children's Hospice. It is the first hospice for children ever in North America and offers respite to parents and a place for families to stay when they visit doctors in the Vancouver area but live far away. The parents know their children will never grow up. Knowing that they have a terminally ill child, no doubt, devastated them, but they did not give up on giving that child the best life they could in the time that they have left. The mental toughness the parents must have to raise their other children, continue to work, and just get out of bed every day understanding what they will encounter, is beyond comprehension. The next time you think of giving up, consider the battle these parents are facing and the fact that they will fight for their children until the day they die.

You can muster the mental strength to do anything you put your mind to, but you cannot leave room for self-pity, self-doubt, or the what-ifs.

CHALLENGE YOURSELF: PERFORMING UNDER PRESSURE

Any elite athlete needs to be able to focus and perform under all circumstances. To maintain composure and perform at their peak, athletes must find ways to channel their thinking into a positive outcome.

Let's say you are presenting a major proposal at work and are, understandably, nervous. Focus your thoughts on what you do well and what you need to accomplish. If you're doing a large presentation at work, remind yourself of the following:

- You've done your research.

- You are good at public speaking.

- Your ideas are solid

- You are presenting to people who respect what you have to say.

- You are doing your best.

Take a deep breath, and focus your thoughts on the great job you will do because you have mentally prepared for this day. Remember, you only fail if you haven't tried.

KEY TAKEAWAYS

In this chapter, you learned about:

- Signs of mental toughness include the ability to self-monitor, accept the consequences of your actions, and let go of the past.

- Daily habits of mentally tough people are perseverance, hard work, and self-confidence.

- Use visualization techniques daily to help improve mental toughness. This includes picturing where you see yourself once your goal has been realized.

3

NEVER JUDGE MENTAL TOUGHNESS BY ITS COVER

Mental toughness and physical strength are completely different. A man can go to the gym and lift weights every day and be incredibly physically strong, prepared for any physical endurance test that is thrown at him, but that doesn't mean that he would be mentally prepared to deal with something of equal mental difficulty. A great expectation is that physically strong people can deal with anything that they face and that a physically weak person will fall apart at the slightest unhinging, but that is false.

To overcome adversity, one needs to be strong, but that's not possible for everyone. Most people can handle slight disruptions in their lives without falling apart, such as dealing with a difficult coworker, but it takes a mentally tough person to be able to overcome extreme situations or persevere through trying times.

The people that have risked their own health, time, and safety for others, may not look exceptional if you pass them on the street. They may look ordinary, weak even, on the outside, but if you were able to see inside their minds you would see the strength that is exuding within.

I have seen well-built men with loud personalities fall apart under stress and I have seen slight women who are typically not taken seriously, react to stressful situations with grace and strength. The ability to handle adversity and challenges in life has nothing to do with one's appearance so be careful not to judge mental toughness by its cover.

Are you someone who already shows promise of mental strength? Here's how to tell:

1. Confidence: A sign of mental toughness is to be confident in yourself and in your abilities to perform challenges you set

for yourself and in getting through difficult times. Every chance you get, practice being confident in yourself and remind yourself of all that you have done. If you are trying to beat a time in a marathon or climbing the ladder to your dream job, do what you need to do to reach those goals every day; practice makes perfect.

2. Maintain Your Calm: Everyone who exhibits mental toughness is capable of maintaining a calm attitude when things get stressful. Exhibiting mental strength is remaining chill and calm when everyone else is entering panic mode.

   Few people are born with the gift of calm in a chaotic situation; there is much practice that is needed. People who want to build mental toughness need to experience difficulties, within reason, so putting themselves in uncomfortable situations is necessary to build resilience or to be prepared for feared emergencies. If someone is afraid of their children choking, for instance, taking a first aid course and learning how to deal with these situations will help them to remain calm in a stressful situation. Someone that is intrigued by rock climbing but afraid of heights will need to begin with small cliffs and work up to higher climbs to build resilience.

3. Adversity in Life: Someone who has come through extreme adversity in life and had to deal with challenges that are not a normal part of life is mentally tough; they have to be. Overcoming racism, psychological or physical abuse, neglect, growing up in poverty, or other challenges gives you an insight that not everyone has. These challenges give a perception in life that it is possible to overcome tragedy and that small issues are not worth wasting time on.

   When you have not grown up with obstacles in your life, you don't know what it means to fight to overcome adversity.

This, of course, is not something one should be blamed for. We all dream of a life without complications, but it is only those who have had to climb out of the rubble of a broken life, rise above grief, or persevere beyond other opposition that will truly know what it takes to be mentally strong.

EXAMPLES OF THOSE WHO HAVE MENTAL TOUGHNESS

Mental toughness is necessary to thrive in life. There are some people who are expected, by society and their peers, to be mentally tough, but there are others who exude a quiet strength that many overlook.

In society, we often see the elderly, women, and children as weak—often at just a glance. Let's take Drew Barrymore as an example most of us recognize. Today she is a well-adjusted mom of two kids and has a successful talk show, as well as a booming movie production company—but her childhood would have broken most. She was interviewed (*Drew Barrymore*, 2021)and talked about growing up in Hollywood, surrounded by celebrities, and had her first movie break at age five in E.T. Drew was introduced to drugs at a party at age nine and quickly formed an addiction for which she went to rehab at age 12. She was then admitted to a mental facility by her mother at age 13 and was there for 18 months. She fought to be emancipated from her parents at age 14 and won. She has made a wonderful career for herself and has, with daily effort, fought to keep her sobriety.

Barrymore's journey is not something that many adults are mentally strong enough to deal with, but she managed to find the determination and perseverance to remove herself from a life that tried to kill her innocence.

Some other people we underestimate in regard to their mental toughness include:

- Those who give birth: Giving birth is one of the most excruciating events that one can go through. Not only does labor pose physical pain, but there is the psychological element that accompanies the process. She may not be muscular, but withstanding the pain of contractions and the worry of delivering a healthy child is something that most muscular men would not be able to endure. Without mental strength, childbirth would not occur and if not for the incredible mental toughness of those who go through labor, our species would die off. So the next time you see a slight woman with her little one, remember that they are here because of the mother's sheer strength.

- First responders: When you look through history and study the various disasters, wars, terror attacks, pandemics, and other pandamonium, there is one constant - the mental toughness of first responders. When the twin towers fell on September 11th, 2001 and people fled for their lives, stunned, not knowing what had happened, firefighters threw on their gear and ran into the immense black clouds of smoke and debris without a thought for themselves. The mental strength that any firefighter needs to have during a fire or other disaster is unfathomable. They put themselves in danger's way to save humans, pets, and what remains of treasured possessions.

- Medical professionals: Doctors and nurses show incredible mental toughness every day in their jobs but that was ten-fold during the Covid-19 pandemic when they showed us on a larger scale, the sacrifices they were willing to make for the well-being of others. It took incomprehensible mental toughness for medical staff to walk into a hospital and care for those who were not only dying of an unpredictable disease but to do it while knowing full well they were putting themselves at risk of contracting this disease.

WHEN EXPECTATIONS EXCEED REALITY

Never let someone's appearance lure you into believing they are incapable of doing great things. Likewise, don't assume someone who is well-built and has extreme physical strength can handle emotionally charged or mentally anguished situations.

Remember that slight mom I just mentioned? Chances are she can handle tense situations and stress much better than the bodybuilder that spends hours a day at the gym. Lifting weights takes practice and makes you look intimidating, but size has nothing to do with mental toughness.

No matter your gender, size, or age, you are not born mentally tough but it can be earned and learned. It is not the physical girth of someone that makes an impression on this world, but the immense courage it takes for them to fight for what they want and to look at others with the respect that is earned.

The mind is the most powerful part of any one of us. It has the ability to break us or lead us to our ultimate goals. If you allow yourself to believe that someone who is 6-ft-3 is mentally stronger than a 5-foot-tall old woman, that's your assumption and chances are, it's the wrong one.

When you look at Holocaust survivors, many are frail women. These women speak of the children that were stolen from them, the spouses that were shot in front of them, and the torture that they endured. The only reason they are still alive is their own willpower, their own persistence, and their own strength.

To lose a child and carry on living is a great example of mental strength in itself, but to continue living a life where you can help others is a true testament of will. You may not realize it, but one of the most powerful women in the world is also one of the most mentally tough, yet the tragedies she's lived through might be too much for Captain America. This would be none other than Oprah Winfrey.

Oprah explains in her book, (What Happened, 2021) about the early years of her life. Born to a teenage mother, was raised in poverty and eventually sent to live with her grandmother who then raised her. At only age nine, she was sexually assaulted by a cousin. She was assaulted until she was 13 years old, and gave birth at age 14 to a baby boy who died when he was only two weeks old. It was through her child's death that Oprah decided to take back her life, build mental strength, and persevere to the powerhouse woman she is today.

CHALLENGE YOURSELF: BECOME RESILIENT

To build mental toughness, we must go through uncomfortable and challenging situations. To increase your resilience to the uncomfortable, try having a cold shower every morning. This exercise will help build your mental toughness due to physical and mental discomfort.

Taking cold showers helps boost our lymph circulation which helps increase our immune system and endocrine function which in turn helps increase proper blood circulation. A cold shower will help build resilience that will help you become more mentally tough (*Resilience: Build Skills*, n.d.).

KEY TAKEAWAYS

In this chapter, you learned that:

- mental toughness has no face. A child can exude more mental toughness than a grown man. Don't judge mental toughness by its cover.

- mental toughness is possessed by those who have faced adversity and challenges.

- a person who is mentally tough exudes confidence and can remain calm under stressful circumstances.

4

TODAY'S SOFTENED GENERATION

You may be hearing a lot of chatter and the accumulative sound of eye-rolling from older generations as they watch today's youth (and many middle-aged folks) clamor for recognition and sustainability from doing virtually nothing (Hogg, 2021).

Back in the day–particularly before social media took over the world–people had to work hard and get by on their own grit and determination to rise to the top and make a good living. There was a lot of competition and not everyone received a participation badge. Today's youth in particular seems to want it all dropped at their feet while they are live-streaming or dancing their exuberant yet vastly under-talented feet off.

Even the peers of those who feel entitled are seeking retribution for the bad name that has been bestowed upon all youth. There is a majority of today's generation that feel they should be given a free ride based on the fact that they are young and enthusiastic, but many born into Generation Y want to be recognized for their work ethic.

Today we are constantly slammed with the term *influencer* or *content creator*, which basically means their contribution to society is filming TikTok videos or doing make-up tutorials. While these may be entertaining to watch, today's *influencers* are not making any significant changes to our world and are actually making themselves mentally weak.

Exactly why are millennials so soft? Many would say it is due to parenting and the fact that many of today's youth are handed everything on a silver platter because they want their children not to suffer the difficulty of a hard day's work. Others blame society for making it so easy to get by with a wink and a smile. The real reasons that today's youth are so soft could be largely due to the following:

- Everything Comes Easy: It wasn't always easy growing up in the '70s, '80s, and '90s, but as parents, many have failed to provide the basic coping skills to their children. There's no doubt that many young adults today have received awards, own cars, and have more than the previous generation dreamed of, and it is well earned, but not by them. Rather, it was earned by their parents or other societal pressures that created a matrix of evaluations and situations whereby everyone needs to be recognized.

  I am glad to have grown up in a time when you had to earn your worth, your validation, and your recognition. There are changes that need to be made by society and the young adults of today if they want to live a life they can be proud of truly earning, and one that won't disappear as they age.

- Everyone Wins–Even Without Trying: The ego of millennials has a thirst for attention that never seems quenched. It began for this generation with the parents who raised their children as peers and not as people they should say no to. At school, everyone gets a participation ribbon and there are no grades in elementary school but everyone gets a smiley face, gold star, or thumbs up. The times of there being one winner–a single excellence achiever–are gone and it is making for some young adults who have never been told no and have no idea how to actually vie for what they want.

- Validation Generation: Everyone seemingly needs validation in the form of likes or views when it comes to social media. From first dates, weddings, meals, or dance crazes, everyone seems to need validation for every little thing that they do. The days of quietly doing a good job and feeling good about yourself are gone and there are videos of people ordering coffee, live-streaming in Disneyland, and posting every aspect of their lives to be rated and affirmed. The true sadness lies in the fact that with constant posting and pleading for recognition, the ability to enjoy the small moments and feel proud of achievements is lost in the shuffle to seek out others' opinions.

- Expect Wealth for Average work: Working nine to five may allow you to make enough money to get by, but it won't make you rich. Today's youth expect to go to an average job, do average work, and live a good life without budgeting. There have been videos posted by employees at popular coffee chains, restaurants, and other positions that are reacting to a 30-hour week as though they were being held hostage without food or bathroom breaks for that time. Millennials say they can change the world, solve world hunger, and house the poor, but they also expect to do this by filming homeless people shivering while they stare through a lens. Without doing much of anything, they expect adoration and recognition.

- Role Models Are Famous for the Wrong Reasons: Having someone to look up to is fine, but there is a difference between commending the passion of Greta Thunburg or the philanthropic endeavors of Princess Diana and celebrating and idolizing the random "icons" who became popular overnight. Rather than seeking out the issues of the world and trying to make it a better place, by becoming educated on climate change for instance, millennials would rather spend their time streaming YouTube and concerning themselves with who the newest Hollywood star is, maybe dating.

The generalization is that Generation Y is consumed with being validated by others and recognized and praised for things that literally anyone can do with a ring light and script. In the Olympics you don't get a medal just for showing up, yet that's what elementary schools are introducing to our youth. With the expectation that everyone wins for no reason, no wonder we are seeing an influx of youth expecting success to be handed to them on a silver platter.

Society did today's youth no favors by coddling them for the slightest inconveniences and for rewarding them for what should be expected of them. Imagine your boss gave you a raise for all your hard work, but you knew you had been slacking off for the last two weeks. Would you feel that you needed to put in the effort to be rewarded? Of course not! The same message is being sent to youth when they receive accolades for work they haven't done. They expect praise for nothing. There is no need to put in effort to get a reward that you are receiving for doing nothing and the drive will be gone to prove them right.

WHAT IS WRONG WITH NEEDING ATTENTION

It's nice to feel appreciated but constantly vying for notoriety, especially when there is no valid reason, promotes emotional instability and mental weakness. Needing to be validated by others to do anything is a detriment to self-value and worth (Litner, n.d.).

Increasingly, millennials are engaging in sharing private moments of themselves or others and expect others to feel anguish at disheartening moments and to become emotionally invested. Some *influencers* are so convinced that their followers will be distraught without their posts that they make a whole blog or video on how they need to take a break to regain their mental health. While focusing on mental toughness is key to living a successful life, building your whole world on a very public platform is the opposite of having mental strength.

There is an abundance of people who post about or discuss their struggles with finances, relationships, or jobs and eat up the pity that anyone throws in their direction. Their ego is fed, not by the satisfaction they get out of a hard day's work, but by the hollow accolades they receive from people that they often don't even know.

When we seek the comfort or praise of others to feel worth something, we become less mentally tough. Without self-worth that grows organically from hard work, sacrifice, failure, and success, we are not going to gain strength. We gain mental toughness from working through our difficulties and taking accountability for our mistakes, not blaming them on others. We only learn from what we have done wrong if we acknowledge those mistakes and take responsibility for them. It does nothing to brush issues to the side and blame others for what we have become.

There are different types of validation that affect our mental toughness very differently: internal and external validation. Here's the difference (Streefkerk, 2019).

- Internal validation: The feelings of validation that you have toward yourself and your feelings, allowing them to be recognized and accepted. Internal validation means that you give accolades to your efforts and feel comfortable and confident in who you are so that outside judgment and criticism do not bring you down.

- External validation: This is the reliance on the support and opinions of others to validate your worth. You may find it difficult to do much without the encouragement and support of others pushing you forward.

Seeking support or validation from an external source is okay, as long as it does not control feelings we have about our worth. There is a spectrum of validation that people require from outside sources and many are not going to harm your mental toughness, but there are some that rely on external validation, which is very damaging to the psyche and causes mental weakness.

Why Do People Seek External Validation?

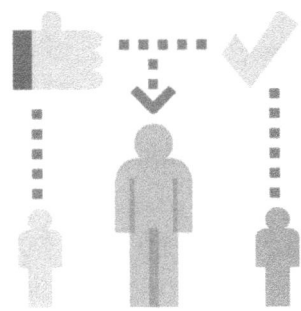

There are many reasons that someone may rely on external validation from others. These reasons include gaining a feeling of self-worth, how you rely on others, and may affect how you act around others.

I believe those who received emotional validation from their parents at a young age have a greater sense of security and emotional cognizance. A child that is given praise and a feeling of worth will grow up feeling that she or he is capable of doing great things.

From my experience, when children are raised in an environment that is devoid of encouragement, depriving them of self-worth, they are less likely to have the ability to regulate emotions. These children may also have difficulty with or be susceptible to the following:

- inability to trust other people

- fear of being rejected

- chronic anxiety

- arbitrary behavior

Studies have linked mental health conditions such as borderline personality disorder or depression, to growing up in an environment where you were not validated.

On the other side, excessive validation and praise can cause children to grow up with a feeling of entitlement and superiority which may make it challenging to have meaningful relationships or relate to others. With constant praise comes a narcissistic personality that can transpire into issues later in life, such as

- body dysmorphic disorder.

- histrionic personality disorder.

- dependent personality disorder.

Not everyone that has experienced excessive praise as children will have these personality traits, but it may resonate with you, in which case, it is a good thing you have this book to help set you on the path toward mental toughness.

Are You Someone Who Seeks Validation?

The balance between internal validation and external validation can shift to an unhealthy balance quickly. Sharing your good news with family and friends is not necessarily a bad thing, but how do you know if you've gone too far to the external validation side?

You may be at risk of needing too much external validation if you do any of the following:

- You have a difficult time setting boundaries

- You find yourself being an overachiever for the praise of others

- You feel guilty saying no

- You avoid conflict

- You take rejection, such as not getting a job promotion, personally

- You post provocative content online for attention

- You feel that you must know everything to be liked

- You gossip constantly to get attention

- You agree to do things you don't want to do so others will like you

- You exaggerate a circumstance to gain notoriety or attention

- You become distressed when attention shifts away from you

- Your quest to gain outside approval becomes all-consuming

- Your view shifts when someone doesn't agree with you

There are many people-pleasing aspects to someone who is seeking external validation and several habits that will lower self-esteem and create rifts between relationships. Becoming mentally tough is going to help heal some of these negative aspects of your life and help you become a more successful and strong-willed individual.

Seeking validation from others steals the power you should be giving to yourself and lends it to someone else, giving them ultimate control over how you feel about yourself. You should never allow anyone else to validate you other than yourself because it steals from what you think you are capable of.

Running to someone else any time you feel you might be making the wrong decision or to see if you are doing a good job only takes away the internal validation you should be giving to yourself as someone who is building mental toughness.

EXERCISES TO STOP SEEKING EXTERNAL VALIDATION

You may have been well aware that you sought validation from others or maybe you have only realized it through reading the last section of this chapter, but either way it needs to stop.

We feel good about receiving accolades for a job well done, and we should, but it should only enhance our pride–not be dependent on it. Someone who thrives on external validation, such as the TikTok influencers mentioned above, demonstrates a lack of self-worth and an absence of mental toughness.

There are a variety of ways you can stop this negative behavior.

1. Explore Your Childhood: Rediscover your childhood and identify different situations or people who may have made you feel invalidated. Did you feel unheard or unattended as a child? What were the situations in which you felt neglected or that you deserved praise that was never given? Some call this exploring your inner child and by doing so, you can discover many things that you were never provided with that are essential to healthy self-esteem and mental strength.

    Once you determine what you never received as a child, whether it be attention, compassion, or praise, then you can begin to give yourself all of those things that you were lacking. As an example, if you did not get praise for working hard as a child, tell yourself often that you are doing a good job and have worked hard to make it as far as you are.

2. Say No: Seeking external validation and doing whatever will please other people is a difficult thing to stop, especially when you are afraid of losing people as a result. Don't worry,

you don't have to go cold turkey, but you do need to make baby steps right away.

Begin by saying no to little things and deal with small amounts of discomfort before moving onto a larger scale of rejecting others. Eventually, you will be more comfortable refusing larger asks, especially when you realize that not everyone—very few in fact—will turn away when they are refused.

3. Practice Self-Validation: Rather than reaching out to others to validate feelings of worth, practice self-validating techniques that empower you. Positive affirmations can help replace negative feelings and self-talk that only serves to debilitate your self-esteem. Remind yourself through self-affirmations that you are enough and that you are capable.

4. Connect with Mentally Strong People: Take a hard look at your support network and consider if they are supportive or if they contribute to codependent behaviors. Does your network support strong ideas and encourage you to work harder or do they encourage you to dwell on the negative and suffocate you with their own issues? A strong support network will support your boundaries and encourage you on the path to success.

5. Deconstruct Negative Relationships: Seeking external validation once in a while to celebrate your accomplishments is okay, but do the people you are reaching out to have your best interests at heart, or are they likely to exploit your personal traumas?

Anyone who will turn your difficulties into their own personal discussions or use them against you is not someone you want in your corner. Internal validation is key to giving you the drive to succeed that you need.

There is a spectrum to external validation. Asking for someone to join in your celebratory moments or asking for advice occasionally is one thing but when it becomes a constant way to seek validation, you need to seek other options for empowerment. Seek internal validation for your accomplishments and take accountability for mistakes and learn from them moving forward.

CHALLENGE YOURSELF: INITIATE A DIFFICULT CONVERSATION

There are times in life when we must decide to have a difficult conversation with someone we have in our personal or work life. Often, people tend to tiptoe around sensitive topics and avoid bringing up conversations that can initiate unfavorable or difficult outcomes.

You may have someone in your life that exhibits many of the traits that are listed in this chapter. Maybe your sister is always on social media, posting everything about her life and everyone else's and it's made you feel uncomfortable and a bit annoyed. Take the opportunity to sit down with her and discuss how this makes you feel and let her know that you don't want your life spattered across social media for all to see. Her life being a free-for-all is her decision, but it does not apply to you.

If you have a boss that constantly makes you stay late while they leave early several times a week, have that difficult conversation. If running the business as though it were your own is not something you agreed to, it is up to you to have that difficult conversation with them and let them know that it needs to stop.

With any situation that requires that difficult talk, stick to your guns and accept the consequences that come.

KEY TAKEAWAYS:

Throughout this chapter, you learned:

- The expectations of today's youth exceed their accomplishments.

- People crave external validation because they don't believe in themselves. Practice telling people 'no,' practice self-validation, and connect to mentally strong people to avoid seeking external validation.

- Build up your self-worth to build internal validation by giving yourself credit for what you have accomplished, and acknowledging the validity of your feelings.

5

MENTAL TOUGHNESS COMES FROM DOING THE HARD THINGS OVER AND OVER AGAIN

We are blessed to live in an era busting with technological advances, quick weight loss fixes, and recognition for virtually nothing. Convenience has made life easier in many respects but it has also contributed to complacency, especially in the younger generations that were born into this accommodating age. We have already discussed, in the previous chapter, how today's generation receives recognition too easily and without having to try at all, never mind repeatedly.

In a pinch, most people will take advantage of the easy way out, but the issue today is that rather than that road being the least traveled, it is downtrodden and broken from overuse. It seems that most people want to put in the least effort to make it big in life and reap the rewards of hard work that they don't necessarily want to put in.

The recognition that many seek via social media is a great example of doing little with the expectation that great things should be received. Posting a 3-minute video harping about someone that ruined your customer experience or posting a verse of a song expecting to be the next Taylor Swift is not realistic. The trouble with today's society is that everyone expects to succeed with minimal effort.

Mental toughness is built through trial and error, dedication to hard work for desired results, and not giving up despite the turmoil. There is very little worth having that comes from little effort and everything worth going for will come from determination and grit.

Getting a promotion requires you to spend extra hours in the office well after others have gone home. Graduating at the top of your class means doing extra research on a term paper or studying for an exam well after you feel comfortable with the material. Losing weight is more than popping pills or starving yourself; it is about exercising regularly and feeding your body with the necessary nutrients to flourish.

Going the easy route will only make you reliant on other people or on supplements, but putting in the work necessary to achieve great results on your own will help you build mental toughness. Through failure and resurrection, you will become reliant on yourself and grow confidence in your abilities to get things done. No one that has earned their success has ever gone the easy route and those who have clawed their way to the top have shared common traits.

A large part of what makes someone mentally tough is resilience. Being able to deal with difficult situations such as relationship issues, financial distress, or health issues is what makes someone resilient. Just as we can build our mental toughness, resilience is built up of different situations that we overcome. It is the ability to thrive amid adversity and the ongoing perseverance that one shows.

We don't all consciously become resilient—in fact, it's not often something we set out to do. Some people are thrust into challenging their toughness due to a circumstance or occurrence that they never imagined could happen to them.

For example, a young mother who visits the doctor with a complaint that she is exhausted from caring for her children finds out that she actually has cancer, and this is the cause of her energy depletion. This is not a scenario that a happy young mother imagines, but it's now something that she needs to deal with. Accepting that this is your place in life is not easy. In fact, it builds mental toughness. Fighting the disease that is trying to steal your life is what builds resilience.

Another example that haunts me is the families that were forever changed after the terrorist attack on September 11th. There were many people that were challenged and rose to the occasion of becoming resilient through extreme trauma and change, including spouses who lost the loves of their lives, parents who lost children, and children who lost parents. Those left behind had to pick up the pieces of their lives and work through the emotions that were forced upon them. Everyone affected by that day that lived to tell about it was challenged and had to adapt to their feelings of loss, fear, and anger. None of those people set out to be mentally strong that day, but all of them needed to be and they rose to the challenge through struggle, hard work, and perseverance of a determined spirit to not let evil win.

COMMON TRAITS OF MENTALLY TOUGH PEOPLE

As mentioned previously, no one is born with mental toughness; it has to be earned through hard work, failure, resilience, and reliance on one's self. As with myself, you may find your true calling through perseverance and resilience. Using the building blocks of a failed endeavor will construct a deeper meaning with a stronger foundation.

Those who build mental strength do have common traits built on habits that they practice each day (Cikanavicius & Juby, 2017).

1. Challenge themselves: Mentally strong individuals seek amends for their mistakes rather than slink into hiding. They grow from their missteps and view obstacles as a way to better themselves.

2. Focus on situations they can control: Mentally strong people will focus their energy on things that they can impact and control. They will not waste time worrying about events that cannot be altered but will hone in on what they can alter or what makes them feel empowered.

3. Set clear and achievable goals: They set goals that are clear and attainable and strive to reach them each day. They get

up in the morning with a set structure of what they need to accomplish and focus their energy on reaching these milestones.

4. Champions of change: Those who are mentally strong are thrust into constant adaptation, especially those in roles of leadership, so they need to be flexible. These individuals often have contingency plans in place for the possibility of future change that may occur within a company, establishment, political party, or another leadership vessel.

5. Use failure to catapult to success: Anyone in a position of power, and individuals who have done well in their chosen path, know that success is reached through trial and error. Small mistakes are used by mentally tough people to learn from and to turn into greater potential moving forward. There is a risk of failure in everything we do and not all of our endeavors will be successful ones but it is what we do with failure that truly leads to success.

6. Dissolution of fear. Fear leads to missed opportunities and stunts the fire that could be used to thrust us toward our dreams. Many people put off changing jobs, asking for a raise, pitching an idea, going on a trip, and truly living their lives because they are afraid to fail. We all must seek our dreams and then make them happen so that our list of regrets is limited to what we couldn't do, not because of a lack of trying, but because we needed to amend our path.

7. Exude confidence: When you are confident, you are more likely to try new things and rise to the challenge of tasks that are more intricate or difficult for others to try. When you exude confidence, others believe that you can take charge and are trustworthy to do what needs to be done, therefore you are more likely to be chosen for a job, as part of a team, or as a go-to person for your boss.

8. Receiving constructive criticism: When you are mentally tough, you are able to handle constructive criticism well and utilize the advice to make things better. If you get insulted when someone gives you feedback on your performance, practice listening and digesting the comments. You don't have to follow all advice, but listening to what others have to say will open you up to a world of good.

9. Practice dismissing toxic people: It is challenging to exclude people from your life, especially family members or friends that you have relied on for your whole life, but there comes a time when you need to consider if these people really have your back. When someone puts down one of your ideas without any helpful advice or shows remorse for your good fortune, practice walking away from that relationship or at the very least, limiting your contact with that individual. Mentally tough people surround themselves with positive and like-minded individuals, not those who create drama.

10. Work with adversity: True mental strength is derived from overcoming adversity rather than succumbing to it. When something seems insurmountable, take the initiative to work your way around that problem or find another way. Transform an adverse circumstance into a forcefield of energy.

We are all going to face obstacles in our lives, whether they are brought on by circumstance or by what we set out to accomplish. Following through on our ideals and pushing onward despite challenges that seem to be hopeless is what being mentally tough is all about.

GRADUAL PROGRESS IS STILL PROGRESS

When you are beginning to overcome a challenge, you need to start slowly to avoid feeling overwhelmed and giving in altogether. It's okay to build up to things over time, as long as you stick to it and don't renege on your obligations to others and yourself.

Some examples of things you can work up to gradually include

- working out 5 days a week.

- beginning a calorie-deficit diet.

- going back to school to change a career or expand current knowledge.

WORKING OUT

When you have never exercised before or don't do so on a regular basis, it can seem overwhelming to engage in physical activity multiple days per week. To increase your chances of success, determine your goals and build from there, whether it be weight loss, training for a triathlon, or getting fit for life.

Say your goal is to work out five days a week so that you can become fitter. You are going to exhaust yourself and fatigue your muscles if you go hard from day one, and from zero to five days is not realistic. Instead, set a time limit for when you want to be at your optimal goal of five days a week and then build from there.

For example:

- Goal: Working out five days per week within one month

- Week 1: Work out Monday, and Wednesday

- Week 2: Work out Monday, Wednesday, and Friday

- Week 3: Workout Monday, Tuesday, Thursday, and Friday

- Week 4: Workout Monday, Tuesday, Thursday, Friday, and Saturday

Setting clear and attainable goals will help you reach your ultimate destination without feeling overwhelmed or like you are failing.

CALORIE-DEFICIT DIET

If you want to lose weight, you need to reduce calorie consumption so that the calories you consume during the day do not exceed the calories you expel (Frysh, 2021). Cutting calories too much right off the bat will lead to hunger and other adverse effects that could result in you giving up your goal altogether. Instead, if you are planning on lowering your caloric intake from 2100 to 1800 per day, do so little by little. For example:

- Week 1: Cut 100 calories per day

- Week 2: Cut 200 calories per day

- Week 3: Cut 300 calories per day

By the end of the 3rd week, you will be down to your optimal calorie intake and it will have been gradual enough that you won't have felt hungry or that you are giving up too much.

GOING BACK TO SCHOOL

Some jobs require that you keep up to date on current statistics, styles, or curriculum, or you may even want to change your career altogether. Going back to school can be expensive and time-consuming which makes it an unlikely resource for anyone who has significant financial obligations, but it isn't impossible for those who are capable and willing to put in the work.

If you are upgrading a degree or changing careers altogether, there are several courses available online and most can be done in your own time frame so you are not giving up your main source of income while you better your chances of making more money. If you take a course or study for a career change online, make sure you set out specific times that you will work on your studies so that you don't push them until later in the day and then run out of time altogether. Having a set schedule will help keep you on track.

Progress is progress, and some people are able to get to their goals quicker than others, depending on a variety of factors, including:

- Financial obligations such as providing for their family

- Personal responsibilities such as children

No matter what obligations you have in life, you are going to get to your end game if you have a plan and determination. Setting a deadline for when you want to complete your schooling, open your business, or change careers, will help you keep a steady pace in developing your ideas and reaching your planned opportunity in a timely manner. Not setting a deadline can prolong the time it takes to reach the outcome since there would be no time limit, which often leads to procrastination.

CHALLENGE YOURSELF: WHAT WAS YOUR MOMENT?

This may be difficult to address, especially if you have put the past to rest, but think of what initially gave you the knowledge that you were mentally tough or what will catapult you from tragedy to triumph?

Most people who search for mental toughness or that have gained mental strength, have dealt with adversity, trauma, or another painful situation that has introduced a need to gain strength or collapse into themselves.

What was the moment that made you strong? Did you go through a divorce? Were you severely injured and needed to claw your way back to health? Did you lose a loved one too soon in your life and struggle to carry on? It doesn't matter if it was hard or if you felt pain; all that is normal. What does matter is that you didn't wallow in self-pity and you dug yourself out of a difficult time and rose to the challenge of carrying on.

KEY TAKEAWAYS

In this chapter, you learned about:

- Gaining recognition and finding success without trying is what makes today's younger generation soft.

- Mentally tough people share common traits, such as using their mistakes to learn, challenging themselves, exuding confidence, and working through adversity.

- For success, you must set a goal and move mountains to get there.

6

YOU HAVE TO CHOOSE YOUR HARD

Life is a series of challenging and difficult tasks, decisions, and events, no matter which path we choose (Meinschein, n.d.). It's up to each chapterindividual to determine what hard means to them. It can be way more difficult to live with the consequences of being broke/unhealthy than to put in the effort to become successful/healthy. In other words, the price you will pay for not making your dreams come true is far greater than the one you will pay if you do.

Hard work goes into building a solid career that pays well, owning a beautiful house, and raising a family. You cannot take time to slack off or someone who is harder working will step in and take over with their work ethic. It is a decision that you make every day to work hard to live a good life.

You can thrive and live your best life or accept the *easy* way out and struggle in this life. Believe it or not, there is difficulty required for both of these paths, but only one allows you to reap the rewards of prosperity and mental strength.

The Difficult but Prosperous Path

There has to be a plan to follow the path that leads to prosperity and mental toughness. You cannot go out into the world hoping for the best and expecting it to happen without putting any forethought into it.

It's typical of human nature to follow the path of least resistance, but that path is crowded and worn down and leads to the same place as everyone else who settles for mediocrity. But if you are eager to thrive then there are some ways you can travel along the path to success.

1. Why is it difficult: What part of what you set out to do is difficult? Do not tell yourself that it is impossible because there is nothing that cannot be done without determination. Figure out what is difficult and then go about doing the things that can be done more efficiently so that by the time you get to the really hard part, you can see the goal line.
2. Go step by step: Often, when we think of something that needs to be done, we consider the end result and do not take the time to acknowledge that one larger task is only something that is obtained by taking several smaller steps. Instead of looking at the big picture, decide what you need to do one bit at a time so that the task feels much more doable.
3. Know your end game: What do you want to walk away with at the end of the day, task, or event? Know what that looks

like. If your goal is to own a coffee shop, you can't just rent a building, throw in some coffee machines, and expect it to flourish. First, you need to draw up a business plan and have a clear idea of what you want your business to look like and how you will help it grow.

If you want to run a triathlon, you are not going to show up the day of the event and expect to finish in record time or without shin splints. You will need to set out a training schedule and build up your stamina and strength.

When you choose to go after what you want in life, you will need to work hard for it and continue to work hard to keep what you have earned. Anything worth having does not fall into one's lap, but is earned through a continuously strong work ethic and mental toughness.

The Difficulty of Choosing the Easy Path

There is actually nothing easy about not putting the effort into yourself or your future. When you don't put in the effort to eat healthily and take care of your body, you are leading yourself down a path that will lead to health problems such as heart disease, diabetes, and obesity, which leads to a host of other issues. When people do not take care of themselves, they are essentially limiting their potential by allowing their bodies to become neglected and wither away.

When someone chooses to ignore their physical health. It may be easy to go through a drive-through for dinner on a busy day, or not exercise at all because setting an exercise routine is too difficult, you are denying yourself the basic needs of your body. When we don't eat well and take in the proper macronutrients that our bodies need, we are limiting our potential. Exercising and eating healthy support many necessities of life, such as:

- Good sleep patterns

- Emotional wellness

- Stabilizing moods

- Providing ample energy

- Lowering the risk of chronic diseases

- Cognitive clarity

- Sharpened decision-making skills

Your future will reflect the effort you have put into it. If you work hard, you will be more likely to have financial stability than if you put in minimal effort to just get by.

TURNING YOUR HARD INTO A FUTURE

Determining your future is one of the most difficult decisions you will ever make. What will it look like? What will you do? Will you work for someone else or will you start a business and be your own boss? No matter which path you choose, it will be difficult in varying ways.

Someone that chooses to work while upgrading a career will need to put in great effort and time management skills to ensure their future will lead to greater things. By working hard by day to pay the bills and putting themselves through school and attending school and doing homework by night, the hard work that is chosen will lead to a prosperous future. That is the hard thing they chose.

On the other hand, someone that doesn't want to work more than they have to might have a job that just pays the bills. But when the time comes to pay for an emergency, such as car repairs or medical bills, or if they are laid off due to lack of job security and have no savings, their hard will come in the form of trying to pay the bills, possibly taking out a payday or personal loan that they can't pay back and finding themselves falling deeper into debt. That is the hard thing they chose.

If you want to start your own business, you need to take into account all of the factors that go into that decision, such as determining:

- What type of business will it be?

- What will make it unique?

- How will others be able to identify your brand?

- What is your business structure?

- How will you market your business?

- Who is your customer base?

- What are your start-up costs?

- Will you take out a loan or will you get investors?

- Where will you open your business?

- How many employees will you need?

- Where will you get your supplies or products from?

You will also need to determine your accounts, brand, distribution, marketing, competitors, accounting, and other factors that go into running a business.

If you would rather be an employee, then you have other factors to consider, such as whether you go into a field that allows you to climb the ladder or a profession like teaching where you will happily sit for the rest of your career. Deciding to be a lawyer, teacher, doctor, electrician, or work in retail, all require different types of hard work. You need to decide which hard you are willing to embrace and then give it your all.

No matter what you choose to do with your career or yourself, it should be hard because you should be putting your entire effort into it. Life isn't easy no matter what path you choose, but it can be more rewarding depending on what you put into it and the mental strength you gain along the way.

HOW DIFFICULT IS YOUR CHOICE

Without thinking about it, we all choose our paths in life, work, and love. If you find yourself in a situation where you feel worthless, it might be time to ask yourself a few questions. Just remember that the grass may look greener on the other side of the office, in someone else's yard, or across the world, but what is it that you are genuinely ready to work hard for?

Is it time to switch jobs? Ask yourself some questions, such as are you excited about work or do you dread going in every morning?

- Is your work affecting you on personal time?

- Are others noticing that you are not happy in your job?

- Are your ideas dismissed at your work?

- Is it difficult to make ends meet based on your wage or salary?

- Has your mind been wandering to thoughts of another job?

Leaving a job that is not fulfilling is hard, but so is staying at a job that makes you feel like you are getting nowhere. Which hard are you willing to commit to based on the questions above?

Are you in a relationship that is stripping you of self-esteem? It takes a great deal of mental strength to leave a relationship, but it is just as difficult to stay in a commitment that is not going anywhere. If you feel you need to put your relationship into question, consider if it's time to leave your relationship:

- Does your partner submit you to physical or emotional abuse?

- Does your partner have a history of deceit?

- Has your partner been unfaithful?

- Does your partner see you as someone who has value?

- Is there mutual respect between you and your partner?

- Have you experienced feelings of unfulfillment in your relationship?

- Is there more give than take between either one of you?

- Is a lot expected of you in your relationship? Do you expect a lot?

When there is an imbalance in any relationship, whether platonic or romantic, there are going to be issues. While relationships take work every day, they should not be continually one-sided or make you feel as though you are missing out on something better.

CHANGE YOUR PATH

You need to reevaluate if you are struggling, whether it's with weight, your job, family and friends, or just life. If the struggles you are going through right now offer no reward at the end of it all, you need to consider if all the effort is worth it or if you should change your path.

For example, changing a job or making a career change is difficult, but if you are not happy where you are currently, or if you are barely paying the bills, or have two jobs to get by, then you need to consider changing your work. It's not easy to go to school and work to pay the bills but neither is working exhaustively for very little reward.

One of these difficult choices leads to years of struggle with no end in sight while the other will be challenging for a time, but there will be a goal and a deadline for you to begin seeing improvements in your finances and your mental state.

CHALLENGE YOURSELF EXERCISE: ARE YOU ON THE RIGHT PATH?

The great thing about life is that we can always change our direction in life if we aren't satisfied with where we are headed. Many people know the path they are meant to be on early in life while others struggle to find exactly where they belong.

To determine if you are on the right path to living your best life, ask yourself the following questions:

1. Are you happy in your job or career?

2. Have you decided to only have relationships with those who you respect and who respect you?

3. Are you setting new and more beneficial habits for yourself?

4. Do you often reevaluate your life?

5. Is there something that you look forward to?

Consider the answer to these questions and see if you need to make any adjustments so that you can answer yes to them all.

KEY TAKEAWAYS:

In this chapter, you learned that:

- The difficulties in chasing your dreams are far more rewarding than the grief of not trying at all.

- Your path to fulfillment and happiness should be through hard work and perseverance.

- When you doubt the path you are on, ask yourself if you are happy, content, and fulfilled.

7

THINGS YOU NEED TO BE AWARE OF WHEN YOU'RE STRUGGLING

A n unsettling part of life is that we all go through adversity, but it's how you handle that adversity that sets you apart. Mental strength is the difference between accepting that challenges help shape who we are versus giving in to them and letting them weigh us down.

It is easy to feel that you are alone and that no one else has ever felt exactly as you do now (Costas & Denney, n.d.). There are many marginalized groups that, understandably, feel they are never going to find the support they need. Some of these groups include:

- members of the LGBTQIA+ community

- people going through divorce

- parents who have lost a child

- immigrants struggling to adjust to a new country

- victims of domestic violence

- those who struggle with clinical depression

Going through something life-altering makes someone feel isolated and it can be too painful for them to reach out. When you are struggling in life, it helps to remember that you are not alone in your journey of pain or disappointment. Everyone goes through victories and losses, which is what makes this life so precarious and wonderful. While it would be wonderful for everyone to flourish and for there to be no pain in this world, the fact is that for all our planning, we still have moments where we struggle.

Things you need to be aware of when you're struggling include

1. No One's Life is Without Sadness: Life is imperfect no matter who you are or how much you have. It's important to remember that the darkness you are going through right now is not going to last forever and that happiness is inevitable.

2. You Won't Always Struggle: Whatever you are going through right now, will pass. Whether you are going through financial difficulty, are arguing with a spouse, or arguing with friends, it won't always be this way.

3. You Don't Need to Suffer Alone: Reaching out to a family member or trusted friend when you are going through something serious in your life does not mean you are weak. It is okay to ask for help or have someone listen to what you need to get off your chest.

4. Acknowledge Your Feelings: Whatever you are feeling, no matter how unpleasant, acknowledge those feelings and what they mean to you. If you ignore how you are feeling, you will only make things worse later on as they will resurface. Giving your feelings a place will help keep them from coming back later on.

5. Turn Your Struggles Into a Lesson: Using your struggles as an opportunity to learn and grow is a stellar move. Most successful people built their empires on the stepping stones of mistakes and struggles throughout their journey.

6. Acknowledge All That You Have: It is easy to become bogged down with the negative in life and overlook all that we have. To remind yourself that these struggles are temporary, write down in a notebook, every day, all that you have to be thankful for so that you have a visual of how blessed you truly are.

7. Switch Your Mindset: The struggles you are going through are valid, but when we focus too much on the negative we can feel that what we are going through is insurmountable. Knowing your struggles and making a plan to move beyond them is productive. But fixating on these issues is only going to make things worse.

8. Everything Happens For a Reason: We may not understand what it is, but everything happens for a reason. Every challenge presents an opportunity for growth and change for the better, but sometimes we have to create the reason ourselves. As long as we don't dwell on the negatives in life, we can embrace the highs and lows of our every day that make life as memorable as it is. It is an unrealistic expectation for everything to always go as planned, so take the challenge and turn it into success.

9. Your Struggles Are Valid: It can be disheartening, and even annoying when you are expressing your challenges and someone takes it upon themselves to express their own journey. It is expected that if you share your experiences, others will do the same, but it's important to remember that your issues are valid, no matter what someone else's experiences may be. The important thing is not to dwell on

what we are struggling with while also giving them the validation they deserve.

ANY OBSTACLE CAN BE OVERCOME

With few exceptions, all obstacles can be overcome. There can be impediments that lead to a dead-end street in one avenue of your path, but there is always a way around it. Find a solution that will act as a bridge to get you back on the right track to where you need to be. For some, this may be delaying progress in opening their restaurant because of a hold-up with the building contractor. This does not mean that all is lost, it gives one more time to prepare for when the day arrives and possibly get other things done that they were going to wait to do.

The first step to overcoming obstacles is to identify them and absolve them. If you do not take the opportunity to acknowledge any impediment, you may

- feel frustrated that good fortune evades you and someone else always gets the same good luck.

- experience overwhelming thoughts that you will fail until you believe it.

- have feelings of inadequacy that you could have done better if you did not lack the ability, intelligence, or conviction.

- feel jealous and angry that others are thriving while you struggle.

- find that stress has a significant negative effect on your mental wellness.

- experience conversations that loop in your head about what you think you can achieve and wish others would know.

Taking these few examples of how succumbing to obstacles can affect your life, learn what to avoid and use the following strategies to overcome obstacles and become more mentally tough and successful.

DEFINING YOUR OBSTACLE

Is your obstacle a perception or reality? No obstacle is insurmountable, yet our minds often make us believe that they are. Our minds often warp the severity of the obstacle depending on our current mental state, position in life, and how many obstacles we have overcome.

If you have recently dealt with an emotional blow, such as a friend being rude to you, then being rejected for a raise or promotion may seem very personal when it is not. If the same rejection came at a time when everything in your life was going well, perhaps it wouldn't seem like such a blow to your ego. We often perceive the severity of an obstacle based on what we already have going on at the moment.

CHANGING HOW YOU PERCEIVE YOURSELF

Often, obstacles begin with our lack of self-confidence and what we believe we do and don't deserve. When you believe many of the challenges in your life come from within, it means you have a negative view of yourself. This way of thinking needs to change.

Make a list of all the words you would use to describe yourself, then cross off any negative words that you have written down. Moving forward, think of yourself in the positive light of your own words, without any of the negative. The first step to overcoming obstacles is believing that you can and if you think ill of yourself, you aren't going to have much of a chance. You need to know that you are capable of moving beyond what is holding you back.

BELIEVING IN YOURSELF

People are often afraid to move beyond the rut they are stuck in because they don't believe they can do better or they do not deserve better. Overcoming obstacles is going to happen when you envision what you want and believe that you can get there.

If you want a better job, a house with a picket fence, or to travel around the world, envision yourself there and then make the small steps it takes to get to that point.

SETTING CLEAR, ATTAINABLE, AND MANAGEABLE GOALS

I have discussed goals previously, and we are going to discuss them again. Taking steps toward your goals is critical, but to get there you need a map of where you want to end up. The goals you set need to be clear to you and those around you so that there is no abandoning them. You may need to be redirected occasionally or take a step or two back, but the path to what you want should always be marked. Other ways to reach your goals include:

- State them clearly: Say you want to become more self-aware, for example.

- Make them achievable: Set goals that can be achieved, not ones that are so far-fetched you will not be able to attain them. An achievable goal would be to make more money within the year. An almost unattainable goal would be to become a millionaire in the next year when you have $100 in your bank account.

- Make them measurable: Rather than saying you want to lose weight, say how much weight you want to lose and then set a timeline for when that goal will become a reality.

There are some life-altering obstacles that no one can go through unscathed, such as the death of a loved one, divorce, or the loss of a job. Understandably, these losses can make one feel hopeless. It is also through these obstacles that people find their true mental strength and rise to new levels of determination. Many will turn their devastation into a way of motivating others to overcome their challenges.

MENTAL STRENGTH IS USING ADVERSITY TO BUILD SUCCESS

Impossibility is not in the vocabulary of someone who has built up their mental toughness. There are many examples of people you know to be successful now, but who at one point faced insurmountable odds only to come back stronger than ever.

WILLIE NELSON

Few country artists are as beloved as American country music icon, Willie Nelson, who has achieved accolades for over 60 decades. According to Forbes (Erb, n.d.), Nelson ran into trouble with the IRS after his accountants failed to pay his taxes properly for years.

After his financial downfall, Nelson took any job that he could, including a commercial for H&R Block, and managed to pay his debt to the IRS. He continues to record and tour, gaining popularity as one of the most popular country artists to this day.

MARTHA STEWART

On the Today Show (Kim, 2017), Martha Stewart opened up about some of her experiences, including prison. Martha Stewart worked her way through college. She is now an author, a home and garden icon, and she partners with Snoop Dogg on *Marth and Snoop's Potluck Dinner Party*. One of the most poignant aspects of Martha's life is that she became the world's first self-made billionaire all on her own.

Martha's namesake company went on the stock market in 1999, but only five years later, she was arrested and convicted of conspiracy in the case of ImCone. She was in prison for five months and fined 30,000 dollars. Many people would have fallen to their knees and pleaded innocent, but not Martha. While she always maintained her innocence, she went to jail without complaining and began knitting and crocheting for the other inmates. The knitted poncho Martha wore out of jail on her day of release was made by one of the other females sentenced to time in prison with her.

WALT DISNEY

Okay, one impossibility might be to find someone in North America (and most of the world) who doesn't know who Walt Disney is and the wondrous world he has created. According to Biography, he didn't step into success, in fact, his first animation studio in Kansas floundered and failed (Tate, 2012).

Walt Disney left for California and gained more success with Disney Bros. Studios, where he really made a name for himself—and a few of his closest friends, such as Mickey Mouse.

MALALA YOUSAFZAI

The most inspirational of all is Malala Yousafzai, born in Mingora, Pakistan in 1997. Malala said that she tells her story (*Malala's Story*, n.d.), not because it is unique, but because it is a common plight for many Pakistani women.

Her father ran an all-girls school in their village and Malala loved the opportunity she was given until the Taliban took over and banned many things, including girls getting an education at school. Malala began speaking out in Pakistan against the unfair treatment handed down by the Taliban. In 2012, she was shot in the left side of the head by a gunman who boarded the bus she was on. She woke up in a hospital in England and was told about all of the people who had heard of her story and wished her well.

After several surgeries and rehabilitation, she became known around the world as an advocate for women in Pakistan and was the youngest person ever to receive the Nobel laureate.

The first instinct of the four, now-famous people, above was not to curl themselves into a ball and admit defeat. They addressed their problems, made amends with the past, and propelled themselves toward success using mental toughness.

CHALLENGE YOURSELF: OVERCOME OBSTACLES

Sometimes, there are obstacles that you can not overcome, such as a chronic illness, being laid off, or having a spouse leave you. When you are left with something you cannot fix, you may feel lost, angry, and even depressed as a feeling of helplessness invades you.

When there are circumstances that you have no control over, focus on something that you can control to help you deal better with the loss or situation, such as:

1. Chronic illness: You may have lupus, diabetes, or fibromyalgia which makes you feel exhausted on a near-daily

basis. This is something that can be managed through a doctor, but in large part, there is little that can be done to fight frequent bouts of extreme fatigue where you may find yourself in bed for most of the day. To maintain motivation, read a book series that gives you something to look forward to, or start writing a journal or that book you have always put off.

2. Made redundant at work: Rather than stay on the couch watching television all day, take an online course to upgrade your skills so that you can find a new, better job that you love.

3. Recently single: When someone decides they no longer want to be with you, it can be devastating. Rather than focus on what could have saved the relationship or why your partner stopped loving you, focus on the ones that love you and will always be by your side.

These exercises to promote mental strength and help you overcome obstacles can be challenging in the beginning, but if you keep at it, they will come as second nature, and soon you will be on the path to a new and exciting adventure and a refreshed view of how strong you can be.

KEY TAKEAWAYS

In this chapter, you learned that

- through difficult times, you should remember you are not alone.

- any obstacle can be overcome by someone who is willing to adapt to issues that arise rather than give in to them. Take away the power of an obstacle by identifying the issue, recognizing why you need to adjust your goals, and then use a different path to get to your desired destination.

- to avoid succumbing to obstacles, you must change how you perceive yourself, believe in your abilities, and set clear and attainable goals.

8

START WITH THE MOST DIFFICULT TASK

P rioritizing your tasks throughout the day will help you be more productive, and the most generative hours are over the first couple of hours of the day. Naturally, our productivity is highest in the peak hours of the morning when we are freshly awake and full of vigor as we enter our workplace or set up at home, so this is when the most difficult or important tasks should be performed. If we wait until later in the evening, our minds are not as sharp and our urgency is overcome by tiredness from making decisions and thinking all day. Completing difficult tasks early in the morning allows you to focus before the business of the day has truly begun.

Completing the most challenging and unpleasant task of the day first will also give you a feeling of accomplishment and, often, can make you feel as though there is nothing you cannot accomplish for the rest of the day (*Hardest or Easiest Work First? What the Research Shows*, n.d.).

Prioritizing the most difficult task early on may look something like:

- Someone looking for a new job may apply for three new jobs before leaving their house in the morning.

- A reporter may check in with the local news or police department before leaving for the office.

- A student may want to go over a chapter in their textbook before going to campus for their exam.

Knowing what needs to be done and carrying through with these good intentions are completely different. It's second nature for many people to pull out their phones and go on social media or watch videos rather than do something more productive. Carring through a difficult task will help you be more productive, remind yourself that it is your opportunity to get ahead in life, make a difference in the world, or get better grades.

Take a piece of paper and write down your most important reasons for doing what needs to be done. It may help you to visualize exactly what you are working so hard for and may help push you through those times you may feel like giving up.

For example, take a second job to save up the capital to open a new business so you can fulfill your dream of being your own boss and following your passion. Or you may have to earn extra money to help support your ailing parents in their time of need. You must write down reasons that are true to your specific situation. In most cases, your reasons may be painful, but don't let that stop you from being honest. I have found that pain has propelled me into making difficult choices that require intense mental strength.

WHY STARTING WITH THE MOST DIFFICULT TASK IS CRUCIAL

Starting with the most difficult task first thing in the day will not only get it out of the way but there are other reasons that we should do the most difficult task first. Mark Twain once said, "Eat a live frog first thing in the morning and nothing worse will happen to you the rest of the day." This refers to people completing the most unfavorable task they have for the day to get it done and then anything from then onward will be more pleasant.

There are some distinct advantages of getting the worst task done first thing in day, including:

1. Our energy is optimal first thing: More challenging tasks take more effort than simple ones; it's basic science. Our circadian rhythm, also known as our biological clock, runs according to our sleep schedule. We are most alert early in the morning, shortly after we wake up, and before we lose steam around mid-afternoon. Since we are more alert when we first wake, it makes sense to focus on more challenging

tasks that take the most energy and demand the most attention.

2. Helps Avoid Procrastination: Putting things off until later in the day, especially difficult tasks, is far too easy. By completing the challenging tasks in the morning, you are bypassing the chances of putting them off until you are too tired to complete them.

3. Ensures the Task is Completed on Time: Often, we underestimate how long something will take to complete. So, by starting the task early in the morning, we give ourselves enough time to finish it without running past the deadline. If we were to begin later in the day, we may run out of time to finish what we need to do.

4. Helps Motivate You to Complete Subsequent Tasks: If you have already knocked the most challenging task off your to-do list, then subsequent assignments will be easily completed.

5. Allows More Time for Important Tasks: You may find that as you begin your first task of the day that unexpected issues arise. You may need to do further research to complete a school paper, or perhaps you didn't have all the information you needed to apply for a new job. When you begin a challenging task early on in the day, there is more time for reaching out for help or getting extra information.

CHALLENGE YOURSELF EXERCISE: EAT THAT FROG

Using Mark Twain's method (Binder, 2018), choose the most difficult or unpleasant task that you have to do in a day and get it out of the way first. Some people say that they prefer completing a few easy tasks that take only a few minutes before diving into a more time-consuming task.

If you are having a difficult time diving into a hefty task first thing, begin with a few smaller chores that take no more than five minutes each. Once the easier assignments are complete, dive into the more challenging job. This way you will have a few items checked off your list and be more motivated to get to work on the more timely assignment at hand.

KEY TAKEAWAYS:

In this chapter, you learned that

- removing the most challenging task from your day first thing will set the momentum for the rest of the day.

- completing large tasks bits at a time can make them feel more manageable.

- doing the hardest task at the beginning of your day will give you a feeling of accomplishment, help avoid procrastination, and ensure the task is completed on time.

9

SUCCESSFUL PEOPLE ARE THOSE WHO ARE WILLING TO DELAY GRATIFICATION AND MAKE SACRIFICES IN THE SHORT TERM

D elayed gratification is almost unheard of in today's age of technological advances and era of instant gratification. Although most people thrive on instant gratification, delayed gratification and impulse control are essential life skills. It may not seem like it, but delayed gratification is the faster way to help realize your goals.

Despite what many people think, you can't get whatever you want as soon as you want it. Instant gratification is becoming a source of frustration because it creates an unreal sense of hope. Delayed gratification allows you to learn from mistakes and work up to what you deserve. But what exactly is delayed gratification?

Delayed gratification is one's ability to resist immediate gratification for an even deeper sense of gratification at a later time. Delayed gratification is correlated to impulse control. Those who have excellent impulse control exceed at waiting for delayed gratification, but this is also a skill that one can develop.

Children avoid disappointment and pain at all costs so they lack delayed gratification. As we age, we become more knowledgeable about the consequences that can be related to delaying gratification to avoid making a poor decision.

When we want something right away without putting in hard work, planning, or consideration, we deprive ourselves of building persistence. This can go back to children getting ribbons and accolades for literally nothing nowadays. All it does when you don't work hard for your accomplishments or wait to feel gratified is weaken your mind and give you a sense of entitlement.

7 TIPS FOR DELAYING GRATIFICATION

There are several ways to help ensure your success with delaying gratification (Cherry, 2020). The top seven ways are listed below.

1. Reward Yourself: Forming a habit is more likely to be successful when we are rewarded for our efforts, including by ourselves. Promise yourself that if you don't go shopping you will allow yourself to buy one new item on your next payday.

2. Practice Mindful Rest: Delayed gratification uses significant willpower and if you are going nonstop, you may find that you burn yourself out before you can complete your tasks. Taking a break to wind down mentally and reconnect with

nature or reading a book will go a long way to assure you have enough energy to complete your tasks.

3. Distract Yourself: You may want a piece of cake but you know that indulging will throw off your diet. Walk away from the temptation and go for a walk, read a book, or start going through your closet to get rid of unwanted items. Often, the distraction will remove the temptation entirely.

4. Is Giving in Worth it?: Imagine you are saving up to buy a house but continually become swayed to spend money on your love of new clothing. Think of the new home you so desperately want and consider if owning a new pair of shoes that will get dirty or buying a new purse that is just as functional as your old one is worth putting off your dream of being a homeowner.

5. Make a Budget: Purchasing items we don't need is one of the main forms of instant gratification. We want to feel happy and reward ourselves with new items.However, we often don't buy what we need, but what we want. Make a weekly budget and once you have reached your limit, stop. Having a budget can help prevent buying items you don't need.

6. Consider Your Merit: What are your core values? Do you need a new vehicle to make yourself happy just because your friend just bought one? Having shiny new things may make some people feel more important, but is that you?

7. Remember the Big Picture: Say you want to skip working out one day because you have better things to do or you think that missing one day won't hurt. While missing one day due to unforeseen circumstances can occur, putting off your health goals one day can lead to repetition. Remember the goal you set for yourself regarding weight loss, what you are

training for, or the health milestone you strive for, and ask yourself if it's worth it to put that off.

THE MARSHMALLOW EXPERIMENT

The Stanford marshmallow experiment (Zacharia & Parent, 2015) that was conducted by a psychologist named Walter Mischel in 1972, is an example of delayed gratification. The study was performed with children that were seated in a room with a tasty morsel of food, such as a marshmallow, and were told that if they were able to resist the treat, they would get an additional snack as opposed to eating the one treat right away.

Many children ate the treat as soon as the person conducting the experiment left the room, but other children resisted the temptation and reaped the rewards of an additional treat.

The results of the experiment showed that the children who resisted the initial offering and waited for the additional reward had many advantages over those children who did not demonstrate delayed gratification. The children that demonstrated restraint performed better academically and had elevated social skills, fewer substance abuse issues, and fewer behavioral issues.

Some additional examples of delayed gratification include:

- Career: Avoid going out late the night before a big presentation so you can feel well-rested and do a good job.

- Relationships: Rather than aggressively confronting your partner and engaging in an argument, you use communication skills to find a dignified resolution.

- Money: Resist making unnecessary, substantial purchases and instead save up your money for a larger purchase such as a car, vacation, or deposit on a house.

- Health: Resist the urge to eat something unhealthy and feel pleased with your decision later on and avoid a sugar crash.

EXERCISES FOR ENGAGING IN DELAYED GRATIFICATION

As with dieting and exercise, it is tempting to jump in all at once and deny yourself anything enjoyable to build up delayed gratification, but like anything, it pays to begin gradually. Do not deprive yourself of the small rewards that you have promised yourself after you have demonstrated delayed gratification.

Try the following steps to engage in delayed gratification for yourself:

- Begin Small: Perhaps you are trying to cut back on eating dessert because it has become a nightly habit. Rather than going cold turkey, try not eating dessert one night a week, then the next week skip dessert two nights, and so on until you are down to eating dessert once a week.

- Set Rules: Perhaps you have a habit of online shopping but then have buyer's remorse. Rather than purchasing something as soon as you see it, sleep on it. If you can't stop thinking about the purchase, then you should consider buying it. Another option might be to go into the actual store, when you can, to make sure you try the item on and genuinely like it.

- Be Grateful: Practice being grateful for all that you have to train your brain to thrive on delayed gratification. When you acknowledge all that you have, including new clothes, a car, and a home, you will realize that new items aren't necessary.

- Remember Why You're Doing It: When delayed gratification becomes difficult, remind yourself why you are doing it. If you are cutting back on spending, remember the house, the trip, or the car that you are saving for

We all want to be happy and believe that we are deserving of things that make us feel elated, but we often give into instant gratification for quick rewards rather than holding off for a much higher reward that comes with delayed gratification. To simplify, think of the children that passed up the opportunity to have two treats but took the singular treat for fear of missing out. Knowing about the marshmallow experiment now, you would likely hold off on eating the singular mallow. Why then would you cave to temptation knowing that something much greater was waiting for you just around the corner?

CHALLENGE YOURSELF EXERCISE: DELAY GRATIFICATION

Think of a big-picture item that you want. Are you saving for a trip, a new car, or perhaps you are saving for a wedding? Whatever you are squirreling money away for–most of us are saving for something–keep that image in the forefront of your mind. Whenever you go to spend money on something that you don't really need, consider if it is bringing you closer to your big-picture goal or if you are seeking instant gratification. If there is nothing to gain from the money being spent elsewhere, tuck it away in a jar, a drawer, or a separate bank account and you might be surprised to see how much-delayed gratification saved you.

KEY TAKEAWAYS:

In this chapter, you learned that:

- successful people use delayed gratification as a reward tool by resisting the temptation of an instant reward, knowing there will be a better reward if they wait.

- delayed gratification teaches us patience and the value of working hard now for a bigger opportunity down the road.

- there are daily ways to improve your delayed gratification skills through daily exercises such as delaying unhealthy actions, being optimistic, focusing on what you are able to do and accepting variability.

10

MOTIVATION AND MENTAL TOUGHNESS

Motivation can be fleeting, depending on our energy levels, our mood, what else is going on in our lives, and other fluctuating factors. What motivation boils down to is discipline, and like mental toughness, it is a learned trait.

When we learn self-discipline, we teach ourselves how to lead a more gratifying and productive life. With discipline comes the ability to make better decisions and create pathways that lead us to a more prosperous life mentally, physically, and emotionally. Discipline allows us to prioritize what is most important when reaching our goals and living a more fulfilling existence.

You may want to do everything at once when planning your future, but it needs to be taken step by step. When you focus on everything at once, you lose track of what you have done and what still needs to be completed. You wouldn't begin a meal by mashing the potatoes; they would be raw and hard. This also applies to building mental toughness. You won't be decisive and strong until you work out what you need to leave behind and work toward.

There are key strategies that can be implemented to strengthen self-discipline and create mental strength and powerful results in your personal and professional life.

DESIGNATE BLOCKS OF TIME

Set aside blocks of time each day or week to work on your goal, depending on what it is. If you are writing a book, set aside a 1-hour block of time each day to write, and little by little, you will be 28 hours into your book by the end of the month.

If you are clearing out a space in your home, carve out 15-minute increments of time each day to remove the first object of clutter that you see. This also works well with reorganizing and cleaning your home. When you walk into a room, tidy the first mess that draws your attention. At the end of the week, you will have spent nearly two hours tidying up or reorganizing.

REMOVE DISTRACTIONS

If you are trying to finish a report for school or work on a proposal for work but find yourself turning on Netflix or reaching for your phone, remove the distractions or remove yourself from the area where the distractions are.

Set up your workspace in a quiet area of your home that doesn't have a television and place any distracting items, such as your phone, well out of your reach or in another room. Rather than growing tired of your task at hand and reaching for the remote or going on social media, take a breath and redirect your focus to the task at hand. Gradually, your workspace will be a place where distractions are not even considered; it just takes time.

GIVE YOURSELF A BREAK

While chasing our dreams, we may make mistakes, such as cheating on a diet or abandoning our workout routine, but dwelling on this will do no good. Despite our best efforts, we have off days, and there is always a chance that life will throw a curveball that we need to dive in for. The important thing is that we forgive our indiscretions or lack of effort and move on. Tomorrow is another day.

EAT THE FROG

You know what this means! Procrastination is all too easy when a monumental task needs to be done. Rather than perplexing over it all day, dive into the worst or most demanding task that you have early in the day so that you can focus your prime energy on it and get it out of the way and make room for more pleasant or less frustrating tasks later on.

THE IMPORTANCE OF REPETITION IN DISCIPLINE

Repetition is crucial when we want to make significant improvements within ourselves or in our lives. Before you know what to repeat, you need to identify what it is that you want to change, improve, or strive for, and only then can you change the paradigm of what has been holding you back.

A paradigm is defined by Webster's Dictionary as, "Example, pattern. Especially: an outstandingly clear or typical example of the archetype."

A habit is formed by repeatedly and consistently doing something, such as biting your nails or eating junk food every night before bed. It may begin as something that you only did once or twice but as the weeks go on, it becomes more embedded in your subconscious and before you know it, you are down to your cuticles and pulling out chips from the pantry as part of your bedtime routine. Implementing good habits and reversing bad ones takes the same repetition and consistency.

If you want to eat healthier, you are going to change more than your eating habits and the foods you eat. You need to change the paradigm or pattern and habits that you are used to when it comes to eating. Changing a paradigm cannot be done with self-restraint alone, but there are two ways that you will be able to change it:

1. emotional impact

2. repetition

Emotional Impact refers to something that is so life-altering that you will never be the same. This is generally due to something negative occurring or, less frequently, something more positive occurring.

Repetition requires you to introduce yourself to something new. It is not necessary to have the information set to memory, but close your eyes and imagine the idea coming to fruition in your subconscious.

It is distinctly important to keep repeating these steps every day to disrupt the paradigm that is embedded in you. Once a pattern has ruled the roost for a long while, it has less desire to change than you can imagine. The little devil on your shoulder, called the paradigm, is going to urge you to skip your jogging day when you are heading to the closet to put on your running shoes. You will feel a strong urge to eat that cake when you know you should be reaching for the lettuce instead. There's always tomorrow to eat right and get fit, right? At least that's what the nagging voice wants you to believe.

This is where you need to begin to visualize a new picture over and over again until your subconscious holds onto it and can resist a resurgence of that nagging voice.

The initial image you put into your mind will be weak because it sits in your conscious mind, like a loosely planted flower. With repetitive imagery, the vision will become more deeply seeded in your mind and will become planted in the subconscious firmly.

As the image becomes more deeply embedded in your emotional mind, it becomes stronger and begins to override the previous image that is now weakening and becoming overturned. It is important that you become educated on what you are embedding in your mind because as it becomes deeply rooted, it will become the new subconscious that instinctively kicks in, even when you aren't thinking about it.

When you want to make a change in your life, it is crucial to change the paradigm. For example, if you want to be more consistent in your workout routine, think of yourself as an athlete. What do athletes do? They work out no matter what so they can keep up their rigorous training and hit their goal.

If you are trying to eat healthier, envision the foods that will nourish your body and how creative you can be with adding natural flavors. If you envision desserts as a way to deter yourself, you may actually be planting junk food into your subconscious, which will defeat the purpose.

REPETITION IS THE KEY TO LEARNING

All of us repeat several tasks daily, often without even thinking about it. We get up, brush our teeth, get dressed, make coffee, read the paper, check our phones, go to work, and many other things that just become second nature because we repeat them consistently.

To use repetition to improve discipline, you need to assign a part of every day to alter your paradigm. Every day, allocate some time to visualize in your mind what you want to do to make your life more fulfilling–to improve your mental strength. It doesn't have to be a great amount of time, even just 15-20 minutes each day will help set a new paradigm.

If you want to make your life something that you can be proud of, thrive in, and not merely exist in, spend time every day working toward your goals. Self-discipline needs to be initiated by you. No one else can get you to want something badly enough for you to sacrifice and work hard.

Some exercises to help you build self-discipline include:

1. Meditate: Meditation is one of the best forms of accomplishing self-discipline. Choose a block of time every day to connect to your inner self through meditation and delving into your thoughts. This form of relaxation and connecting with one's self is critical in forming a strong sense of self-discipline.

2. Make Your Bed Every Morning: Doing something as simple as making your bed every morning will help you strengthen your self-discipline. This small task will help start your day off with productivity and will help you feel that you have accomplished something, however small.

3. Morning Exercise: Begin each day with physical activity such as yoga, push-ups, a jog, or anything else that invigorates your body and kick-starts your mind.

4. Avoid Negative Outlets: Mentally tough people do not waste time with negativity. Negative people and outlets that serve as a source of pessimistic energy will only serve to induce self-pity and feelings of inadequacy. Mentally tough people

focus on the positive, what they can change, and avoid self-deprecating people and situations.

CHALLENGE YOURSELF: REPETITION IN EXERCISE

You can apply this to a number of activities (anything that can be repeated) but for this exercise, we are going with squats.

For the sake of preventing injury, follow these steps to perform a safe and proper squat:

1. Stand with your feet slightly wider than shoulder-width apart, straighten your back, lift your arms in front of you, and engage (tighten) your abdominal muscles.

2. With weight bearing on your heels, back straight, head held high, lower into a seated position until your body mimics how it would if you were sitting down.

3. Go back to a standing position.

4. Repeat.

The first time you do proper squats, you want to limit them to about five repetitions of 10 squats. This means that you will do 10 squats in a row then rest for about 20 to 30 seconds and then repeat. That may not seem like a lot, but for the beginning, it's a good amount. If you already do squats, perhaps add more reps or do the squats using dumbbells or kettlebells to add weight.

Repeat this challenge every day, increasing your numbers gradually by 5-10 each time. This repetition will make the squats easier to perform well and strengthen your muscles to do more over time. This type of repetition is key to learning a new skill well.

KEY TAKEAWAYS:

In this chapter, you learned that:

- motivation is the initial spark that sets your goals in motion. Do not forget that motivation is strongly correlated with self discipline.

- repetition and discipline are key to changing a paradigm. Rather than continuing to live in the past, or worrying about what is to come, live in the moment.

- repetition is the key to learning and setting a new positive habit, such as exercising every day, making your bed every morning, or avoiding unhealthy foods.

11

MENTAL TOUGHNESS AND THE UNITED STATES MILITARY

When you think of the United States military, you may assume that the largest, strongest, most intelligent cadets excel, but it is the ones who have mental toughness that finish first.

A member of the military needs to not only function under pressure, but they need to flourish, exceed expectations, and become stronger as they overcome obstacles. It is not muscular strength that will help cadets overcome what they face during training or on the front line, but the mental strength that comes with years of hard work and commitment.

The military is elite in igniting motivation in personnel and having individuals set goals that they work toward through discipline and mental toughness. Paratroopers, rangers, SEALs, and Green Berets need to go through rigorous training and self-discipline to show they are mentally strong. They exercise excessively, have a limited amount of food to eat, have sleep restrictions, and have several various stressors put on them to make sure they have the mental strength to carry on.

There is no doubt that anyone who steps up to be a member of the United States military has to be motivated to do so. No one joins believing that it will be a cake walk, but it is impossible to know how grueling it is without going through the training. This is what separates those who cannot from the mentally tough.

Those who join the military are driven by a love of their country and the willingness to protect their way of life. The training that goes into the cadets taps into their loyalty and willingness that they have to fight for what they believe in. Dedication is already a factor in most who join the military and mental toughness will follow with those who follow through on their training.

FOUR STEPS TO BUILDING MENTAL TOUGHNESS IN THE US MILITARY

Mental toughness is built gradually and needs to be done with persistent work and determination. Building resilience and mental toughness is a completely different thing in the military than it is for regular civilians.

When we eat that frog by completing our most hated task first thing in the day, such as going through emails, those in the military are eating a much, much more foul-tasting frog than the rest of us. Not even members of the military are mentally tough right out of the gate. They go through rigorous training to get to where they are physically and mentally.

Here are three steps that the military uses to improve mental toughness (Smith, n.d.):

1. Persistence: Once the initial excitement of a new venture has worn off, it is persistence that kicks in to keep you going toward your goal. Allowing your journey to take a back seat is going to weaken your stamina to cross the finish line. Propel yourself toward your objective every day and keep the momentum going.

2. Habit: We all have habits—some are good and some we need to train ourselves out of. It takes as much time to break a habit as it does to set one and both need daily effort and repetition. When you are setting a new habit, you must repeat the steps every day so that whatever you are trying to accomplish becomes second nature. Exercising every day is challenging at first, but after a few weeks, a habit is set and you feel less productive and lack energy if you don't exercise for a day. Eating healthy sets the same standards of well-being so your body needs healthy foods to keep it functioning optimally.

3. Discipline: The foundation of reaching your goals is discipline. When you lack motivation or energy, discipline is what keeps you going. Wallowing in self-pity will achieve nothing, but working toward your goals of exercising more, eating healthier, and meditating will help you move forward. You may know that you need to jog every day to train for a marathon but it's the discipline of getting up, lacing your shoes, and hitting the pavement that matters. Bruce Lee, the top martial arts expert the world ever knew, learned his craft through all of these steps. He practiced every day without fail and let nothing get in the way of his discipline and mental toughness.

CHALLENGE YOURSELF: GIVE IT YOUR ALL EVERY DAY

This challenge is straightforward, but it takes determination. Take action toward building your dream every day. Don't let a single day go by that you don't work on some part of your plan that will lead you to your destination.

Taking a university course means opening your textbook every day and reading a chapter or making notes. Improving discipline means that you need to apply the initial steps to show up every day and give it everything you've got.

KEY TAKEAWAYS:

In this chapter, you learned that:

- the United States military is filled with mentally tough people, conditioned to withstand grueling tests.

- military toughness is built through conditioning, perseverance, determination, and habitual exercises.

- motivation is what it takes to sign up for the military, or any other physically and mentally demanding post, and perseverance is what keeps you in it when exhaustion kicks in.

12

HABITS OF MENTALLY TOUGH PEOPLE

Realizing your full potential does not mean that you need to take on more challenges and tasks than you already have on your plate. The smarter way to reach your goal is to, not work harder, but work smarter by removing unproductive tasks that can drain your energy and mental toughness.

Those who succeed in life do so by planning their time and their tasks carefully. A successful lawyer is not going to file the same deposition twice; it isn't necessary and it is a waste of time. So why would anyone add baggage to their lives, such as self-pity or fear of change, that will only hold them down.

Mentally tough people know how to delegate their time by prioritizing the most important commitments and tasks first. Below are seven additional habits that mentally tough people follow.

1. Embrace Change: By embracing change, you are inviting unlimited opportunities to come into your life by constantly adapting. If change is something that you dread, you will have a difficult time taking risks and engaging in growth.

2. Avoid Self-pity: The only thing that wallowing in self-pity is going to do is keep you stuck in the bad situation that you are in. Everyone goes through difficult times, whether it's losing a job, losing a partner, or having an illness. When we get lost in self-pity, we become fixated on the problem and are unable to see the solution.

3. Own your Circumstances: A victim mentality is a crutch for those who are mentally weak. They dissolve any power they have over circumstances and their own life and emotions by saying things like, My coworker makes me feel inadequate. You should never give anyone the power to control how you feel. Rather than giving others credit for your actions and emotions, use phrases like, I choose to get up early so I can get a head start on my work, rather than, I have to get to work early. Owning your circumstances and choices is a form of mental toughness.

4. Reserve Energy for What you Have Control Over: Energy spent worrying about what we cannot change is wasted energy. Rather than depleting your energy on what you cannot control, as unfortunate as the situation may be, focus instead on what you can control.

5. Don't Worry About Others' Opinions: There are always going to be those who want to bring you down and this has nothing to do with you or what you stand for. In fact, it has everything

to do with their own insecurities. Mentally tough people do not worry about what others think, nor do they make others feel inferior.

6. Embrace Failure: Now, this doesn't mean that you should purposely fail, but it does mean that you shouldn't be afraid to fail despite trying. When we are genuinely doing all that we can do to succeed, the failures we face along the way can only serve as reminders of what not to do in the future. If you are afraid to fail, you will never take risks that will inevitably lead to success.

7. Practice Emotional Intelligence: Mental toughness and emotional intelligence go hand in hand. You cannot move beyond frustrating times without the ability to deal with negative emotions and turn them into something more positive.

WHAT MENTALLY STRONG PEOPLE DON'T DO

Time and again, I have heard people declare how mentally strong they are. They insist they are advocates for self-worth and they don't need to answer to anyone because they are confident in their own abilities. These same people then post their lives on social media and thrive on the attention they receive regarding how they look, or what a good job they've done raising their kids or reorganizing their pantry.

Sharing your life with others is okay, but being fueled by comments, likes, and reposts is not going to make you feel any better about yourself if you are not already solidified in your feelings.

Now that you know the habits of mentally strong people, let's look at some of the things that mentally tough people will never do.

1. Spend Time with Negative People: We all know that someone who is constantly complaining about their lot in

life, other people, or dwelling on some other bit of negative energy inevitably brings everyone down. We should surround ourselves with people and situations that make us feel good about ourselves and about life, not drag us into the recesses of negativity.

2. Give up on Themselves: Mentally tough people do not focus on monetary feelings, but on the goals they are working toward. They do not give up when they face hardships or when exhaustion kicks in. They are fueled by others' lack of belief in them and they will not let anything, not even failure, stand in the way of what they want.

3. Assume They Will be Disliked: Whenever a mentally weak person meets someone, they assume that they will not be liked. The negativity that engulfs them makes it difficult to believe that anyone could love, appreciate, or respect them enough to spend time with them.

4. Hold a Grudge: The emotional and physical damage of holding onto a grudge is more extensive than most account for. A grudge is saying that the negative individual or circumstance that thwarted you in some way is still in control of your emotions, validation, or success. Mentally strong people avoid stress and holding onto a grudge can cause an abundance of stress and result in high blood pressure and can lead to other detrimental emotional damages.

5. Count on Others for Happiness: Mentally strong people do not gauge their success or happiness on the accolades of others. If they feel good about what they have accomplished, they will not allow anyone to steal their good vibes. On the other hand, if someone is super enthusiastic, they won't allow this to go to their head.

6. Do not Limit the Success of Others: Those who are truly mentally strong do not rely on the downfalls of others to help them feel good about what they have accomplished or to make themselves feel better when they are down. They know that comparing themselves to others isn't going to make them a better or worse person.

7. They are Void of Hope: Weak-minded people are often referred to as pessimists. They constantly believe that they are doomed for failure, and that good things happen only to other people and never to themselves. They are so stuck in a negative loop and they whine about their disadvantages in life but never do anything to help boost their odds.

BUILD RESILIENCE IN MENTAL STRENGTH

Whether it be from a person or on the news, a mentally strong person doesn't let negative people or things limit their outlook. Fixating on the state of a failing economy or investing every waking hour in a war overseas that cannot be controlled by our government, let alone an ordinary citizen, is a waste of our emotional resources. A mentally tough person avoids giving energy to what they cannot change.

Below are some exercises to help turn stress into resilience:

MAKE ANXIETY WORK FOR YOU

Our minds are fascinating things. According to Simply Psychology, depending on how we manipulate the brain's plasticity, we can be either an anxious wreck or we can teach it to reassess a circumstance and reframe our mental state to make more beneficial decisions.

By reminding ourselves that all emotions, even anxiety, have a place in propelling us to a better place, we can motivate ourselves to move forward. For example:

119

- Fear, if we allow it to, can trigger a negative response that paralyzes our ability to focus on anything else and eliminates our accessibility to change. Or, fear can encourage us to take a pause and reflect on why things didn't work out for us before and allow us to create an alternate direction that leads to opportunities.

- Anger is a powerful emotion and can debilitate your potential. It can also heighten your attention and remind you what your values and goals are.

- Worrying about things can lead to procrastination as you may want to prolong the perceived inevitable rather than dive in. If we embrace our worrying thoughts, we can adjust expectations and set a goal that is more attainable and realistic.

- Frustration can stunt your potential or make you quit before you complete a task. Instead, use it to challenge yourself to find a way to move around the challenge despite the struggle.

- Sadness is something that we all experience in our lives, but it's how we deal with it that matters. We can let this emotion steal our motivation or we can use it to reimagine our lives and goals to change our circumstances for the better.

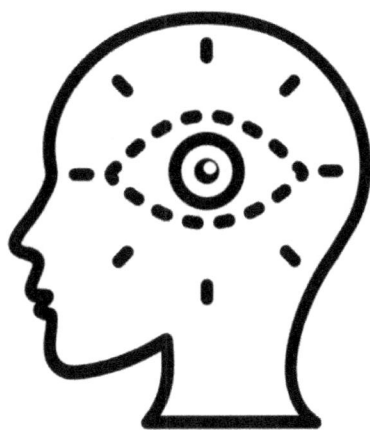

It's human nature to worry about things such as whether we did a good enough job at work, if we passed our test, or if our children are going to be happy. What you can do to build mental strength is to rephrase those thoughts to visualize an outstanding scenario for all of those questions. Your children are happy and loved and successful. Your job loves you and you will get that raise or promotion, and the test that you're worried about? You aced it!

You may think that setting your hope so high is a recipe for disaster, but it actually helps build the expectation that you have for yourself and your life, which allows you to go for what you want unapologetically and with gusto.

3. Get Outside

Getting out in nature is one of the best things you can do for a mental reset and to gain mental clarity. Not only will you get much-needed fresh air, but the distractions at the beach, park, or anywhere you enjoy being, are just wildlife and organic scenery. Giving yourself the opportunity to get outside every day will help make space for your thoughts, even if they are only quietly telling you to relax.

CHALLENGE YOURSELF: VISUALIZE YOUR BEST LIFE

At the beginning or end of every day, envision what your absolute best life looks like. Envision your house, those you love, your job, and where you live. How do you feel about yourself and the decisions you have made today that will move you closer to your best life? Work on altering your decisions and thoughts to envision what you want the story of your life to look like as the book closes.

KEY TAKEAWAYS

In this chapter, you learned that

- mentally tough people share a commonality in their determination to adapt, such as they don't worry about what others think, avoid self-pity, and embrace change.

- mentally strong people do not give up on themselves, spend time with negative people, or hold grudges.

- you can turn stress into resilience by embracing fear as a chance to reflect on what you can change, or use frustration as a challenge to find a way around the problem despite the struggle.

13

THE ABILITY TO FOCUS AND VISUALIZE YOUR GOALS

Consider your favorite athlete mounting the pitch, taking to the ice, or getting ready to compete in the CrossFit games. Now, do you think they are considering how they can mess up or how so many variables could shift beyond their favor? Of course not. Instead, they are focusing on the outcome that they want, whether it's hitting a home run, defending their goalie, or hitting their rep max.

Could you imagine your favorite team telling each other they were feeling a loss coming on or weren't sure if they were going to play well at all? Obviously, you wouldn't be rooting for that team. You want to cheer for the ones that visualize a win and have the mental strength to pull it off.

People who want to do well focus on the positive outcome and have no room for the negative. Just as we should not have a plan B lest we will use our valuable energy resources on thinking up a secondary plan, we need to envision the best-case scenario with everything we do.

We accomplish what we believe we are capable of. When we see ourselves failing at writing our first novel or we don't believe we can run a mile without breaking from exhaustion, we bring those visions to reality. Challenge the way you see the outcome by visualizing the steps you need to take to accomplish those goals gradually. Nothing worth having comes all at once, but we do need to envision the big picture.

In the last chapter, I listed visualizing success as a way to build resilience as strength, and the same applies here. When you focus on what you want and visualize your intended goal, your chances of success are greater than if you imagine failure.

WHAT EXACTLY IS VISUALIZATION?

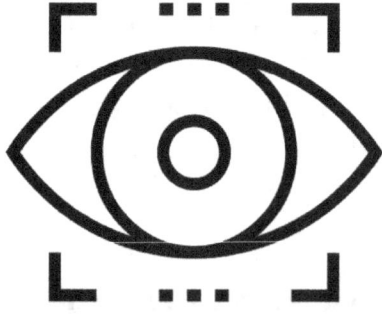

Visualization is a common technique that can be used to help you focus on some event that is important to you. When you have practiced visualization every day, you will help determine the outcome of the speech you will give, the test you are taking, or the marathon you are about to run. Visualizing the intended outcome will help you grow more confident in your abilities and it can promote a more favorable outcome.

Some people think that by considering all negative scenarios they are running out the bad ideas and bad luck, so to speak, so that all that is left is success. We now know that isn't the case and the negativity that circulates through your mind before you go for a job interview or go on a first date can harm the experience.

Running with the idea of the first date, instead of thinking about all that can go wrong—such as losing a button on your dress shirt, spilling water across the table, or running out of things to say—consider all that can go right. Imagine having a wonderful time, being funny, and finding humor in anything that does go awkwardly wrong.

Visualization can make you more eager for what you want. For example, your dream is to move to Los Angeles, so how can you use visualization to increase your yearning to move to the City of Lights. You begin to watch 4K videos on YouTube, or flip through TikTok or Instagram at influencers that post local pictures. Having these visuals will help your goal of moving to LA in your conscious and subconscious mind.

There are many benefits to using visualization techniques, such as:

- Increasing confidence and believing that you are able to achieve all that you visualize for yourself.

- Visualization is a technique that anyone can use, regardless of who they are or what they have and it doesn't take any special skill,just practice.

- When you visualize the path you will take to succeed in life or love, including all you need to do to get there, you will realize those steps leading you to where you want to go in reality.

ACHIEVING YOUR GOALS THROUGH VISUALIZATION

Visualization is something you can use to promote success in every aspect of your life. From opening your own business to making new friends, visualization will help you prepare for and help execute these plans. According to a study in the National Library of Medicine, many highly successful and effective individuals use visualization unwaveringly to help achieve their goals.

Our minds are extremely powerful and, with focus, can help us not only believe that we can accomplish certain things, but can help give us the perseverance to get them done. The ability of our mind is only limited to what we are able to visualize.

Beginning your own visualization journey is simple using the following steps:

1. Choose a Goal: The first step of achieving your goals through visualization is to know what you want. Choose one thing to focus on and begin visualizing how you will get what you want. Visualize the job you want, your health goal, or any one thing you are passionate about and that is what you are going to focus on. You may have several goals and dreams but visualize one at a time or you will not have a clear pathway to success.

2. Visualize Exactly What You Want: Picture exactly the scenario you want to occur. Focus on every single detail in your mind, leaving everything to your imagination and holding it there in your mind's eye. The more detail you can

muster, the more likely success will follow. When you picture the scene in your vision, what are the colors that you see? What do you smell? Is it cold, warm, or hot in temperature? Use all of your senses to bring to life what you are visualizing so it feels like your thoughts surround you.

3. Visualize Each Step of Your Journey: Let's say you are training for a triathlon. Picture every step, from the starting line as you dive into the ocean to begin your swimming portion of the race. Who is standing on the shoreline cheering you on? Imagine the people clapping as you come out of the water and get ready for the cycling portion of the triathlon. What is the weather like? How do your legs feel as you transition from the water to a bike? Imagine dismounting the bike and taking off your helmet as you begin the last, running portion of the race. Visualize the rush you feel and how you can keep going on forever. Imagine the finish line and the crowd cheering as you come across the line victoriously.

4. Visualize Your Goal Daily: If your triathlon is one month away, take time out of every day to visualize the entire triathlon to completion and continue up until the day of the triathlon. This doesn't mean that you need to go through the entire 3-hour race, but run a cliff note version of the key milestones including great detail. Running through the triathlon each day will train your mind to visualize success and bring it to fruition. Visualize your swim stroke, the road you are cycling along, how you will handle the hills, and the speed and technique you will use for the final running leg of the journey.

5. Visualize this journey while you are driving, jogging, or anytime during the day that you have time to focus completely on this technique to better train your mind to expect success.

VISUALIZATION TECHNIQUES

Visualization is a technique that helps bring dreams to reality by training your mind to believe that what you are envisioning will become reality. A mind is a powerful tool that is malleable and can promote success through habitual thinking.

Below are some tips to help optimize your visualization techniques:

- Choose a Quiet Place: For visualization techniques to be fully effective, you will need to do them in a quiet place and without distractions. It takes away from the exercise if you need to regroup or refocus your visualization with every interruption.

- Use an Image to Induce Visualization: If you are saving money to go to Scotland, it might help to keep a photo of Edinburgh Castle near where you do your visualizing. This way you will have a head start in the emotional and mental picture you want to paint for yourself.

- Write Your Goal as if it is a Mantra: Writing a short sentence that represents what you want to visualize will help keep the goal in mind. For example, if you are trying to change your diet to promote health, you could write, "I will eat healthier to be healthier."

Making headway toward your dreams is difficult if you don't use visualization to see clearly what it is you are striving for. Take time each day to focus on your goals and see them clearly in actuality.

CHALLENGE YOURSELF: MAKE A MAP OF YOUR FUTURE SUCCESS

A fun visualization come-to-life technique you can use is making a success map. This map should have a detailed list (in map form) of all things you need to do to make it to your ultimate goal. This map will lead you straight to realizing your goals.

KEY TAKEAWAYS

In this chapter, you learned that

- top athletes focus on the outcome they want to see at the end of a game or race, not what they are afraid might go wrong. We accomplish what we believe we are capable of.

- achieving your goals through visualization is a powerful tool. Visualization techniques allow you to see, taste, smell, and feel exactly what you want your outcome to be. When you focus on what you want and visualize your intended goal, your chances of success are greater than if you imagine failure.

- your mind is a powerful tool that is malleable and can facilitate success through implementing positive habits. When using visualization techniques, choose a quiet place, use a detailed image to set a scene, and repeat your goal as though it were a mantra.

14

MENTALLY TOUGH PEOPLE NEVER QUIT

Those who are truly mentally tough never quit. They learn from previous mistakes and then make things happen. The common theme throughout this book is that mental toughness can be learned and that it is a common trait among those who have led a challenging life.

We are not born with mental toughness but the circumstances that we face in life ignite a fight or flight mode and we can either collapse under the pressure of adversity or overcome them and allow them to strengthen us through the lessons they teach.

Just as mistakes can help us become more successful, trying times help make us stronger. You could say that building mental strength is similar to Charles Darwin's theories of survival of the fittest and natural selection. Those who are willing and able to adapt will survive and thrive.

Being mentally tough doesn't mean that you have to imagine a monumental accomplishment for yourself, it means that you need to dive into everything you do with persistence and honor. Many people who are mentally strong fight through obstacles with the goal of surviving, only to realize that, once they are through to the other side, they have an abundance of knowledge to share with others.

Some people choose to be mentally tough to accomplish their goals, but others are thrust into a life or position that they never asked to be in and have to find strength just to survive. Children never ask to be put into situations that require them to build mental toughness before they even know what it means, but the harsh reality is that sometimes it happens.

The world is full of mentally tough people from all backgrounds who go on to lead extraordinary lives, but being mentally strong doesn't mean you need to live your life in a large way. Some of the strongest people chose to live a quiet life, while others thrive in the spotlight or use a larger platform to promote positivity and live life to the fullest despite hardships.

Some of these notable people include:

- Charlize Theron: To most, Charlize Theron is an actress born in South Africa that is known for her roles in movies such as Monster, Mad Max: Fury Road, and Atomic Blonde. What you may not know, according to multiple outlets including Biography, is that the actress had a volatile childhood with a father that was an alcoholic and beat Charlize and her mom frequently and made threats against their lives. One day, when Charlize was only 15 years old, her mother killed her father during a fight ("Charlize," 2019).

- Charlize's mother was found not guilty due to self-defense and continued to raise her daughter. Charlize struggled through school, didn't fit in, and had chronic health issues. Eventually, the actress found her calling in acting and although she doesn't speak much on the topic of her upbringing, she is a true example of someone who rises out of a terrible situation and becomes mentally strong enough to realize their dreams.

- Stephen King: This world-renowned author is known as the King of Horror but he grew up extremely poor, raised by a single mom who struggled to make ends meet, and faced countless rejections well into his adult years. King, who was rejected by countless literary agents, tossed his first number one bestseller, Carrie, into the garbage because he was convinced it would be discarded like all his other novels. His wife dug Carrie out of the trash and convinced him to send it to agents.

- It was only through decades of perseverance that Stephen found his niche in the darkness of horror writing and millions of fans that crave his twisted, dark tales. If not for mental strength and determination, none of us would have classics like Misery, The Shining, or The Green Mile.

- Keanu Reeves: There are few Hollywood actors as beloved as Keanu Reeves. His films, such as the Matrix, have captivated generations, but it is his backstory that makes him mentally strong. Keanu grew up in Lebanon, raised by a single mother after his father left when he was only three years old. His mother remarried four times and Keanu moved around often as a child. Keanu had to find mental strength that many cannot when his 8-month-old baby died, followed by the love of his life. He also helped nurture his sister for years as she battled cancer. Through all of these challenging times, he remained strong and resilient, donating to charities and being a pillar of strength for those lucky enough to be in his circle of friends and family.

- Bethany Hamilton: While surfing in the waters of Hawaii, Bethany Hamilton found herself fighting for her life at only 13-years-old. A shark bit off her left arm and she nearly bled to death. Rather than let this horrendous attack deter her from her dreams, Bethany was back on her surfboard one month later and continued to practice what she loved. Just two years later, at age 15, Bethany competed in the Explorer Women's Division of the NSSA National Championships and won first place. The incredible courage and mental toughness that it took for Bethany to get back in the water is outstanding. She had to accept that a shark took her arm and she had to adapt and persevere with only one arm, but she wasn't about to let it steal her dreams.

NEUROSCIENCE BEHIND PERSEVERANCE

Perseverance is what differentiates those who win and those who quit. What is it that kicks in during difficult times that separates those who can and those who won't? In part, we can put it down to dopamine—a chemical in the body that helps you feel motivation, enthusiasm, excitement, and accomplishment ("The Neuroscience," n.d.).

Dopamine keeps us motivated and working on achieving our goals. Dopamine can be increased through habitually challenging and changing your behavior. According to Psychology Today, researchers have linked increased dopamine levels to forming habits such as perseverance.

Neuroscientists have done research to determine the link between dopamine and the reinforcement of good behavior and perseverance and good habits.

Dopamine and the link it has to propel one to their goals is not new to neuroscientists, but what has been recently found is that dopamine directly correlates with good and bad habits. This was found in a study that determined key receptors for the production of dopamine acted like a pathway to the formation of habit-forming behavior.

Research done in the field of neuroscientific research shows that significant levels of dopamine might be the differential between someone who perseveres and someone who is more likely to give up. While dopamine is not the only propelling factor in perseverance, it has a significant impact.

We all like rewards. The dopamine reward system works through an intricate structure throughout the brain. This system gives us a feeling of happiness, contentment, or excitement after such things as eating, resting, or being with friends. Dopamine travels through your brain and gives you a feeling of satisfaction as a reward for something that you have done, thereby making it something that you want to continue working on.

This system is used as a warning of types in the animal kingdom. Animals seek out what makes them feel good as a way to avoid pain. The animals in nature seek the greatest reward and, in turn, are rewarded by affirmation in a sense of security. As humans, we seek different rewards than a lion would, but it is all on the same spectrum of how we respond to a task or incident in hopes of a return of gratification.

PERSEVERANCE MEANS NO SAFETY NET

There has never been a successful person who had a back-up, or back-out plan, as it should be referred to. Once you have determined your goal, visualized it, and gotten to work making it a reality, there should not be a plan B that gives you an easy out to abandon your goal in lieu of something easier. Perseverance means that you determine your goals and you stick to those goals, dodging obstacles and climbing over roadblocks to get to where you need to be. Having a plan B to fall back on can lower your chances of success significantly.

Historically, the great commanders during times of war would burn bridges they had just crossed or ships that they rode to arrive at their destination as a way to cement their commitment to moving forward; retreat was not an option. This show of determination was to be an example to their troops and to show their resolve and that what they were fighting for was worth battling to the end.

A similar *die-on-your-sword* tactic can be applied by those securing a business loan. An entrepreneur may put up their house as collateral as a show of good faith that they will not default on their loan. This shows the bank, or other lending agents, that they are planning for success. This is also an initiative for the business owner to put in their best effort not to let their business endeavor fail.

There are contingencies that can be kept in place while you are building your dreams that wouldn't constitute a plan B. For example, if you are starting your own business but have a freelancing job that is paying the bills until the main event takes over, that isn't considered you having a secondary plan in case you fail. It's called paying the bills while working hard to achieve your dreams.

Let's say you want to open a cafe with a bookstore attached in the downtown core of your city, only when you get through the business plan and put everything in place to look for a building, there is already one there. This may mean you have to rethink your location or the coffee shop and bookstore combination. Having the foresight to recognize that things can change shows forethought and adapting to that change demonstrates mental toughness. When we are ready for the unexpected, we are less likely to make decisions while emotions run high.

Mental strength means delving into your inner core and persevering despite all the setbacks and naysayers. Our brains are wired to respond to positive interactions and habits, making repetitive good actions something that we begin to automatically achieve.

And as with all who have paved the way to success before you, failure is not an option when you have perseverance. When things are difficult, push onward, burning that bridge so there is no going back. A contingency plan means safety, not failure, as long as it carries you toward your initial goal and doesn't sidetrack you to a plan B.

CHALLENGE YOURSELF: DAILY VISUALIZATION FOR PERSEVERANCE

It's easy to give up on your dreams and to allow perseverance to fall. But you're here because you want to build mental strength and succeed at your goals, so challenge yourself to maintain the drive to succeed by engaging in these exercises.

ALTER YOUR PERCEPTION

The only thing that is keeping you from reaching your goals is the belief you have in yourself. Change the perception that you have of your abilities and the chances that you will succeed. You will only reach your goals if you toss statistics and probabilities out the window. This is on you and you are capable of succeeding.

TURN CHALLENGES INTO OPPORTUNITIES

Perspective is the main challenge in reaching your goals. While one person sees failure as the end game, another will see it as a way to learn and grow. By viewing challenges as opportunities, there is nothing that can stand in your way of success.

MAKE IT ABOUT YOU

When you envision your goals, you need to see yourself in them. If you want to be wealthy and choose a career based on that alone, chances are you will lose focus and motivation pretty quickly. But when you see your future and passion in your dreams, you are more likely to persevere. Envision yourself in your goals daily, making it all about you and your success.

KEY TAKEAWAYS

In this chapter, you learned that

- there is strength in addressing and learning from your mistakes. If you procrastinate about finishing a file for work and hand it in late, next time work on it a bit every day to avoid not completing it on time.

- perseverance is the difference between someone who moves forward through difficulty and someone who quits.

- setting up a plan B gives you an excuse to quit; don't do it.

15

MENTALLY TOUGH PEOPLE DON'T SPEND TIME WITH WEAK, UNDISCIPLINED PEOPLE

Remember when your parents encouraged you to play with everyone at school and not flock to the pretty or popular girl, or the boy that had everyone swooning because he was the jock? While many people will be drawn to *shiny* people, those who seem to have the most curb appeal, you should surround yourself with those that represent who you want to be.

You can look at it as almost a mob mentality, but on a smaller scale. When you think of a teenager with four of his friends trying to get school work done while the other four want to go play video games instead of study, chances are he will go with them and abandon his studies. Now if the roles were reversed and there was one person who wanted to go play video games and four that wanted to study, chances are the one would forgo the games to work with their friends. This is what the sum of five speaks to; a self-help book by Paula Owens. The tendency of people is to go with the majority.

There is a saying that we are the sum of the five people that we spend the most time with. Keeping that in mind, have you surrounded yourself with people of substance, drive, compassion, and mental strength? Or have you gathered a posse of people that make you feel better about yourself because they haven't got their lives together or count on you for external validation?

Everyone you are in a relationship with–from romantic and platonic relationships to those you do business with–should be someone you admire and respect, someone that supports your dreams but has aspirations of their own. There is a reason that you choose to spend the majority of your time with your inner circle, even if it is on a subconscious level.

Self-stimulation: Our minds are like a muscle that grows with the wealth of knowledge it receives. We learn more through our environment, and that includes who we spend the majority of our time with. Seek out people who help challenge your thinking and with whom you can engage in thought-provoking conversations.

Quips and quarrels over political views, world news, and other stimulating conversations are not something to shy away from, but something to encourage. Sitting in a room full of people whose interests are in the Netflix catalog are not going to help you grow as an intellectual.

Healthier Habits: Consider what the outcome would be if you spent your time around people with no motivation or drive to better themselves. You would likely be unmotivated and stuck in a rut that provided mediocrity. The same can be said for being around physically active people who take care of their bodies and minds. Those around us have a significant impact on our habits, including the good, so if you want to become a more health-conscious person, the likelihood of success being around others who eat pizza and soda every day is pretty slim.

If four out of five friends are health conscientious, the probability of the fifth falling in line is much greater than the other four beginning to be careless with their workout routine. If you need the motivation to implement healthier habits, surround yourself with people who will be a good influence.

Greater Self-Esteem: When you surround yourself with people who are always striving to do and be better and encouraging you on your own journey, a deeper sense of community emerges. You don't need anyone to tell you your dream is worthwhile, but having people that believe in you, cheering you along, will give you a greater sense of confidence.

SHOW ME YOUR FRIENDS AND I'LL SHOW YOU YOUR FUTURE

Daniel Stephen Pena, Sr, who is credited with birthing the phrase "Show me your friend and I'll show you your future," is an American philanthropist, businessman, and business coach. His philosophy with this phrase is that people take on the traits of those they most commonly attach themselves to, whether it is family, friends, or coworkers. We adapt to the traits and habits of those around us most.

Many adults don't believe they could be swayed into being like their friends. They believe they have a mind of their own, but it's not entirely true. How many times have you heard someone say that they need to stop hanging out with a certain friend because all they ever do is drink when they are around them? Have you heard someone complaining that they haven't gone to the gym because their brother would rather watch television and go to the movies together?

Just as negative habits and traits that others possess can pass onto us, so can positive attributes. You are a product of those around you and you will become like them so choose wisely who you spend time with. Dissecting who you spend the most time with and how they impact your life is not easy, but if you are determined to live the life that you have chosen for yourself, take accountability for your future and the people who will help shape it.

We don't make friends for temporary measures; we connect with people we enjoy spending time with and who we expect to have meaningful relationships with for decades to come. When you consider those you spend the most time with now, do they hold the same core values as you do? They don't have to be identical, but do they care about others and friendship, and want to succeed in life?

If you get annoyed with the immature antics of your friends now, can you imagine how pathetic the same attitude is going to be in 20 years? People can change and grow, but when you see no growth in your top five friends, it's time to think about cutting ties with them.

There are seven traits of resilient relationships, according to Psychology Today. They are:

1. Active Optimism: Rather than simply hoping things go well, active optimism is believing that there will be a good outcome and taking steps to lead to that outcome. In any type of relationship, this means that you both agree not to say critical or hurtful comments that can lead to arguments and negative consequences.

2. Decisiveness: This is knowing what you want and being strong enough to take the steps to get there. Decisive action leads to mental strength, such as when someone leaves a toxic work environment.

3. Tenacity: This is persevering when you are faced with failure, adversity, or discouragement. This can apply to the relationship you have with your friends, parents, and children—or it can mean fighting for a career or dream.

4. Integrity and Responsibility: Relationships that are built on loyalty and all parties acting with integrity and respect, are likely to be more resilient. This means being completely honest no matter the outcome and then working together to reach a common ground.

5. Self-Control: In relationships, resisting temptation, using impulse control, and using delayed gratification are critical for success. When we practice self-control, we avoid actions that will impact the relationship in a negative way and help implement healthy coping mechanisms.

6. Honest Communication through Connectedness: In a relationship, the feeling that you belong is built through honest communication. This type of communication can help you feel connected to the person, even when the conversation is less than pleasant.

7. Present-Mindedness: When you are present of mind, you are opening pathways for more meaningful interactions within

your relationship. This can lead to open communication and working together in collaboration for something better.

MENTALLY TOUGH PEOPLE ALIGN WITH LIKE-MINDED PEOPLE

Mentally tough people align themselves with those who have similar values. They do not allow weak-minded individuals to waste their time or give them the opportunity to bring them down.

Strength is built with perseverance and a firm understanding of your core values, which let the world know who you are and what you stand for. Likewise, if someone decides you are not worth their time, don't waste your energy trying to convince them otherwise.

EXERCISES TO DISCOVER YOUR CORE VALUES

Fulfillment is gained by living life according to your core values. Personal fulfillment is determined by defining your core values, which will lead you to follow a path in life you believe in and help you make decisions based on what is important to you.

For this exercise, all you will need is a sheet of paper and a writing tool. Next, write down the three paramount things in your life, such as:

- achievement

- accountability

- health

- family

- intelligence

- compassion

- calmness

- balance

- success

- wisdom

If there are other core values that mean more to you, feel free to use those.

Once you have your top three core values, incorporate them into activities that you perform every day. If health is one of the three core values that mean the most to you, then you would make choices each day that promote optimal health, such as eating healthy, meditating, and exercising.

This exercise helps you find joy in everyday life and encourages you to create it yourself. Your life should consist of your core values, including friends that help make you who you are.

It isn't always clear who is going to help keep you on the path to living a successful and fulfilling life versus those who will steal your spirit and drag you down with self-pity. Just because someone is mentally weak doesn't mean they are a bad person, but they could be unknowingly putting you at risk of sliding into the same rut.

Those who are mentally weak often:

1. Dwell on the past: Mentally weak people have a tendency to stay in the past and dwell on mistakes of themselves or of others. As I've mentioned, there is no moving forward in life and out of a negative state if you have one foot in the past. Instead of revisiting what went wrong with their relationship, job, or whatever else ails them, they are steadfast in repeating the same narrative.

2. Trust others too easily: Trust is not a bad virtue, but when someone immediately trusts people in their life, or even strangers, a host of adverse situations can arise. Trust should be earned by everyone, not given simply because they are someone you happen to know. Anyone can put up a facade about their happy life and moral values initially, but it's how those same people act behind closed doors that will define their core values. Someone who is overly trusting can be easily influenced by others with ill intent and can even be coerced into dangerous situations by shady people. Those who are mentally weak have the views and opinions of others easily impressed on their minds.

3. Over-analyze situations and people: Not everything needs to be analyzed. There are aspects of one's life that should have careful forethought—such as buying a house, choosing a partner, deciding to have children, and other life-altering events—but not everything needs to have so much thought put into it. Analytical thinking is detrimental because it keeps us stuck in the past, in a place that we regret with decisions we wish we never made. When someone overthinks what they could have done differently or puts too much forethought into an event coming up, they are wasting time on something that literally cannot be changed. Take the time to think about the right decisions, analyze monumental

life moments, and take action to do it right in the future or not at all.

4. Engage in self-pity: Self-pity is a key trait in someone that is weak-minded. It's okay to feel let down by something not going your way, but feeling sorry for yourself is not an inevitable response–it's a direct choice. Self-pity is a loop of constant betrayal of oneself. There is nothing good that can come from it because, much like over-analyzing, self-pity is consuming and it becomes easier to revel in the pity of others who may give you attention for your troubles.

5. Become envious of others: Mentally weak people have a tendency to envy what others have, whether it's money, a career, children, or their spouse. They don't put in the necessary effort to improve their opportunities, yet they still wish they had what belongs to someone else.

6. Hold onto anger: There is no point in holding on to anger and refusing to forgive or move on from a negative experience. Holding onto anger has a negative response from the brain and can lead to depression, cause sleep issues, and manifest into physical ailments. Being angry with someone is not something a mentally tough person would do; they would move on and use the experience as fuel to move on. A person who is mentally weak will dwell on and perpetuate the negativity in their everyday lives.

7. Spend time with mentally weak people: Are You Spending Time With the Right People? Are your top five people worth your time? Keeping the principle that we are a compilation of the five people we spend the most time with, do your top five people represent examples of who you want to be in life? You can go so far as to make a list of the people you see most and what you admire about them compared to what you don't necessarily respect.

You may notice the pros outweigh the cons and stand by your current crowd, or you might realize that those closest to you don't have your back or follow the same ethical path you do and it might be time to make some changes.

KEY TAKEAWAYS

In this chapter, you learned that:

- mentally tough people don't spend time with weak, undisciplined people. Mentally tough people align with like-minded people.

- resilient relationships, such as those between mentally tough people, are supportive, honest, decisive, and respectful of one another's boundaries.

- the five people you spend the most time with influence your decisions.

CONCLUSION

Resilience is the keystone of mental strength. It is the difference between someone who bounces back from adversity and someone who is swallowed by defeat.

Do you want to be someone who wades through ambitions but never dives in, or do you want to do more than tread water with your life? There is staying afloat in this world and allowing others to dictate what we can or cannot accomplish or handle, and then there is you telling everyone that you've got your own back and will be all that you please.

Circumstances may throw a wrench in your plans. Use that detour to strengthen your resolve and learn how to put a contingency plan in place so you are not stalled in your future progress. No one is going to become their strongest mentally without having a few setbacks, but you need to look back at your missteps and avoid taking that same path again.

Having mental strength is believing in yourself and the road you have laid ahead of you. Living your best life isn't easy, but remember to choose your hard. Do you want a hard life of constant struggle and disappointment or do you want to work hard to get ahead?

Perseverance and determination are the cornerstones of all mentally tough people. There is no one, regardless of status in life or the advantages they have had, that is given strength. It is more often that those who have struggled greatly and come through challenging circumstances have the power of mental toughness.

BREAKING DOWN MENTAL TOUGHNESS

The power of mental toughness is in you; you just need to unleash your potential. We are not born with mental toughness, but we are born with the ability to learn resilience, determination, and discipline.

Make sure you are steadfast in your goal of empowering yourself with mental toughness by remembering to

- acknowledge your feelings

- focus on health

- externalize your feelings

- work toward goals each day

- assess your challenges

- practice self-compassion

- practice mindfulness

- project how you want to be treated

- choose your company wisely

- eat that frog

We alone are capable of building mental toughness. With every step we take and the boundaries we set, we build our mental strength and embrace the life we deserve.

GET YOUR POWER

The fact that you want to change is already the first step to making a huge difference in the strength you exude and are building.

While others complain about the challenges they face or vocalize their disdain for their lot in life, you are turning your opposition into opportunities and visualizing the life you want, despite the obstacles you may face now.

It doesn't matter where you are in your life; mental strength can be developed and strengthened at any time. Highlight the key points that resonated with you throughout this book and set into motion the plan that you have for using the power of mental toughness.

REFERENCES

6 strategies for overcoming obstacles that hold you back from success. (2020, August 5). Life Hack. https://www.lifehack.org/880737/overcoming-obstacles

7 characteristics of resilient relationships . (n.d.). Psychology Today. https://www.psychologytoday.com/gb/blog/when-disaster-strikes-inside-disaster-psychology/201804/7-characteristics-resilient

Buchecker, M., & Degenhardt, B. (2015). The effects of urban inhabitants' nearby outdoor recreation on their well-being and their psychological resilience. *Journal of Outdoor Recreation and Tourism, 10*, 55–62. https://doi.org/10.1016/j.jort.2015.06.007

Charlize Theron. (2019, October 9). Biography. https://www.biography.com/actors/charlize-theron

Cooks-Campbell, A. (2022, June 2). *What is mental strength? 7 ways to develop more than mental toughness.* Better Up. https://www.betterup.com/blog/mental-strength

Erb, K. P. (n.d.). *Willie Nelson, who saved his career and his house with the IRS tapes, turns 80.* Forbes. https://www.forbes.com/sites/kellyphillipserb/2013/04/29/willie-nelson-who-saved-his-career-and-his-house-with-the-irs-tapes-turns-80/?sh=bd8185855684

Gamma, E. (n.d.). *Brain Plasticity (Neuroplasticity)* Simply Psychology. https://www.simplypsychology.org/brain-plasticity.html#:~:text=Brain%20plasticity%2C%20also%20known%20as%20neuroplasticity%2C%20is%20the

Garvey, M. (2021, February 23). *Drew Barrymore talks about her experience in a "psychiatric ward" at 13.* CNN. https://www.cnn.com/2021/02/23/entertainment/drew-barrymore-psychiatric-ward-howard-stern/index.html#:~:text=Drew%20Barrymore%20was%20virtually%20interviewed%20on%20Howard%20Stern%E2%80%99s

Littlewood, Z. (2016, April 11). *Five Powerful Exercises to Improve Mental Toughness*. Mental Muscle Training. https://www.mentalmuscletraining.com/single-post/2016/04/10/5-POWERFUL-EXERCISES-TO-IMPROVE-MENTAL-TOUGHNESS

Mayo Clinic. (2018). *Fatigue Causes*. Mayo Clinic. https://www.mayoclinic.org/symptoms/fatigue/basics/causes/sym-20050894

Moore, C. (2019, January 14). *Resilience Training: How to master mental toughness and thrive*. PositivePsychology.com. https://positivepsychology.com/resilience-training/

Point of no return. (2022, March 24). Wikipedia. https://en.wikipedia.org/wiki/Point_of_no_return

Ranganathan, V. K., Siemionow, V., Liu, J. Z., Sahgal, V., & Yue, G. H. (2004). From mental power to muscle power-- gaining strength by using the mind. *Neuropsychologia*, *42*(7), 944–956. https://doi.org/10.1016/j.neuropsychologia.2003.11.018

Ribeiro, M. (2019, July 4). *How to Become Mentally Strong: 14 Strategies for Building Resilience*. Positive Psychology https://positivepsychology.com/mentally-strong/

The difference between Mental Health and Mental Strength. (2021, May 24). Hunimed. https://www.hunimed.eu/news/the-difference-between-mental-health-and-mental-strength/#:~:text=Mental%20health%20in%20most%20dictionaries

The Neuroscience of Perseverance. (n.d.). Psychology Today. https://www.psychologytoday.com/us/blog/the-athletes-way/201112/the-neuroscience-perseverance

Bergland, C. (2011, December 26). *The neuroscience of perseverance*. Psychology Today. https://www.psychologytoday.com/us/blog/the-athletes-way/201112/the-neuroscience-perseverance#:~:text=Dopamine%20is%20the%20fuel%20that%20keeps%20people%20motivated

Walt Disney's rocky road to success. (2020, June 17). Biography.

    https://www.biography.com/movies-tv/walt-disney-

    failures

Weingrad, E. (2015, October 27). *Drew Barrymore tells all to*

    Howard in her Stern Show debut. Howard Stern.

    https://www.howardstern.com/show/2015/10/27/drew-

    barrymore-tells-all-howard/

Why Mental Toughness Is Critically Important? (2020). Mental

    Toughness. https://www.mentaltoughness.partners/why-

    mental-toughness-is-critically-important/

Yousafzai, M. (n.d.). *Malala's story.* Malala. Malala.org.

    https://malala.org/malalas-story/